AN ORKNEY ESTATE

To my Mother and Father

AN ORKNEY ESTATE

Improvements at Graemeshall, 1827–1888

GILBERT SCHRANK

TUCKWELL PRESS

First published in 1995 by
Tuckwell Press Ltd
The Mill House
Phantassie
East Linton
East Lothian EH40 3DG
Scotland

British Library Cataloguing-in-Publication Data
A Catalogue record for this book
is available on request from the
British Library

Typeset by
Hewer Text Composition Services, Edinburgh
Printed and bound by
Cromwell Press Ltd, Broughton, Gifford, Melksham, Wiltshire

Acknowledgements

I have received a great deal of generous and valuable help in researching and writing this study. Acknowledgement of the following individuals and institutions gives only partial expression to the gratitude that I feel. My own institution, Nassau Community College, Garden City, New York, has supported my work by granting me two sabbatical leaves, which enabled me to conduct research, to reflect, and to put pen to paper. The National Endowment for the Humanities 1990 Summer Stipend allowed me once again to visit Orkney for another round of research in the Archives.

Over the past several years I have presented aspects of my research to a variety of academic seminars. I am most grateful for the astute commentary I received from seminar participants at Johns Hopkins University, Adelphi University, Columbia University and the University of St. Andrews. I also benefited from participation in the First Annual Dinsmore Homestead Symposium in Burlington, Kentucky.

Several friends and colleagues have been most generous with their time by reading various drafts of this manuscript and sharing with me their commentary. I am most grateful to T. C. Smout, I. D. Whyte, Mary Nolan, Gerald Sider, William P. L. Thomson and Nancy Ellen Jones for their assistance and wisdom in steering me in the direction of clarity and relevance. I must cite for special mention the astonishing and admirable efforts of Dr. R. P. Fereday, particularly since his twenty pages of closely reasoned, learned and single-spaced commentary opened up for me so many fruitful lines of inquiry. I must single out for gratitude the Orkney County Archivist, Alison Fraser, for many years of assistance and advice. Her knowledge of the local historical resources is invaluable, as is her willingness to share these resources with a visiting American scholar, full of innocence about Orcadian ways. I must extend my thanks to the Orkney Islands Council for having the wisdom and the willingness to fund a County Archive, not to mention a full-time professional archivist. Nancy Jones has been my partner in life for decades. This book could not have been written without her encouragement, support and advice.

Contents

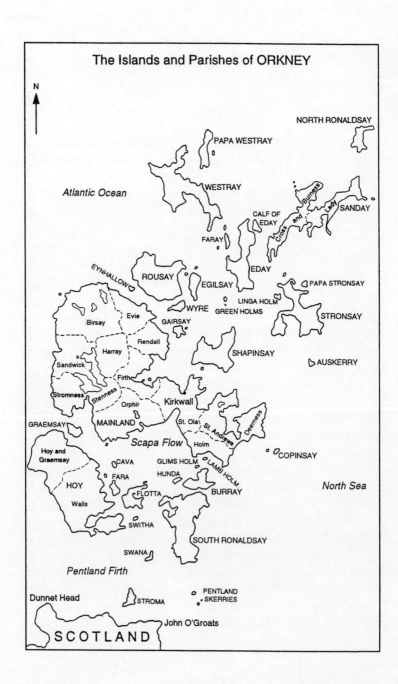

The Islands and Parishes of ORKNEY

Introduction: The Issues at Stake

A cursory examination of the literature on agricultural improvement in Great Britain, and specifically that devoted to Scotland, indicates the need for a more intensive study of local and regional archives. Eric L. Jones has long urged agricultural historians 'to get behind generalizations to the textured reality on which they rest, to find sense in individual truth'.[1] Scholarly studies of particular cases of agricultural improvement in Scotland, whether they scrutinize the estate, the parish or the county, have uncovered a surprisingly variegated pattern. For example, some improvement efforts were doomed leaps into the dark, while others were protracted processes that required the sustained labour of generations to complete. A few were false starts that later reversed course. Some improvements were confined solely to the home farm, but they left the remainder of the estate surprisingly untouched for decades. Finally we encounter numerous sudden bankruptcies, broad- scale and ambitious local agricultural improvements in regions adjacent to the major urban centres, and improvements that merely traced the expanding geographical pathways of commerce and transport.

Since many of our older generalisations are now suspect, I. D. Whyte has observed that 'We know little about the means by which estates were developed, or about the scale and effects of the operations involved'.[2] This study, primarily based on an examination of the papers of the Sutherland Graeme estate known as Graemeshall, in the Orkney Islands, will seek to avoid stereotyped views and achieve the perspective that only comes from attention to detail. It is notable that much of the experience herein described fails to conform to the more general pictures of the improvement process that have been offered.

Scottish historians, who are more comfortable with the term agricultural 'improvement' than with its counterpart 'revolution', note that, despite the efforts of determined pioneers, the process of change gained momentum north of the border decades later than it did in England. T. C. Smout remarked that the 1780s and 1790s were the years of greatest change in the country as a whole.[3] Until the advent of agricultural modernisation, Scottish farming was caught in a vice, having reached its 'climatic limits of expansion under existing techniques' by about 1750, only to have this condition followed by a strong and steady increase in the rural population throughout the country.[4] Though it has been demonstrated that the proliferation of Scottish rural industries, such as linen-spinning and weaving, kelp gathering and burning along the northern and western coasts, and straw-plait weaving by rural women, etc., provided supplementary sources of income for both tenant and laird, there was always the danger that Scotland could eventually become a vast rural slum. Contemporary observers feared that their country might sink into such an impoverishing morass. Yet significant agricultural improvement did occur throughout Scotland, though the pattern was uneven, with striking regional variations evident throughout. Between 1750–1825, the farmed area of Scotland grew by 40%, accompanied by a dramatic 100% increase in overall agricultural productivity.[5] The steady expansion and broadening of market forces throughout Scotland during the eighteenth century was a catalyst for these changes, almost all of which took place in the Lowlands. These were inevitably combined with ever more frequent and reliable commercial contacts with England. In evaluating a process in which he feels that 'regional variations were paramount', Edward Royle observes that 'change occurred unevenly, and in different ways according to soil type, distance from markets and local custom'.[6]

In order to understand this process, we need to address

such essential questions as the agents of change and the methods of implementation. In several cases, absentee landlords inspired and initiated improving endeavours. They also had the additional incentive of increasing their income.[7] For example, Royle has correctly noted that agricultural improvement and enclosure of common lands in Scotland can be attributed both to rising grain prices and the caprice of fashion, particularly the impulse to imitate the lifestyles of the English aristocracy, combined with the uneasy contemplation of the associated expenses.[8] In other instances, the impulse to improve came from the estate factors, or chamberlains, i.e., the estate resident administrators, many of whom were assuming roles of professional property managers.[9] In most cases, however, the factors, lacking autonomy, could do little more than carry out the wishes of their superiors. Finally, so much of the initiative and the investment capital for changes in the Scottish landscape came directly from the pockets of the individual tenant farmer, who fenced and drained his fields, separated arable from pasture lands, selectively bred livestock, and aggressively marketed his product.[10] A common cause of rural disputation lay in the fact that these tenants, much too frequently, were not compensated for such expenses when they, or their descendants, vacated the farm.

The personalities and characters of the improvers, and the relationship between lairds and their factors are topics seldom explored, yet were matters of crucial importance. It is thus becoming evident that the manner in which the actors perceived their roles, their underlying ideological assumptions, and their abilities to work with each other typically affected the fate of improvement ventures. It should be obvious from this study that this proved to be the case with improvements in Graemeshall estate.

Notes

1 Eric L. Jones, 'Afterword', in W. N. Parker and E. L. Jones (eds.), *European Peasants and their Markets* (Princeton 1975), p. 359. Similarly, G. Whittington recently noted that work

on Scottish improvement 'has suffered from over-generalization' in G. Whittington and I. D. Whyte (eds.), *An Historical Geography of Scotland* (London, 1983), p. 145.

2 I. D. Whyte, 'George Dundas of Dundas: The Context of an Early Eighteenth Century Scottish Improving Landowner', *Scottish Historical Review*, 1981, p. 2.

3 T. C. Smout, *A History of the Scottish People: 1560–1830* (New York, 1969), p. 248.

4 Bruce Lenman, *Integration, Enlightenment, and Industrialization: 1746–1832* (Toronto, 1981), p. 116.

5 M. L. Parry, 'Changes in the Extent of Improved Farmland', in M. L. Parry and T. R. Slater (eds.), *The Making of the Scottish Countryside* (Edinburgh, 1980), p. 196.

6 Smout, p. 296. R. H. Campbell, 'The Scottish Improvers and the Course of Agrarian Change in the Eighteenth Century', in L. M. Cullen and T. C. Smout (eds.), *Comparative Aspects of Scottish and Irish Economic and Social History, 1600–1800* (Edinburgh, 1976), p. 252. G. Whittington refers to improvement being 'a fashion in a period when being "progressive" was desirable'. Whittington and Whyte, p. 144. Edward Royle, *Modern Britain: A Social History, 1750–1985* (London, 1987), pp. 2–3.

7 Campbell, p. 206.

8 Royle, pp. 2–3.

9 Adams, p. 160.

10 Royle, p. 2.

CHAPTER ONE

The Orkney Islands
and their Transformations

The Orkney Islands, separated from the Scottish mainland by the swift-flowing tides of the Pentland Firth, were several decades behind the southern Scottish counties in the timing of local agricultural improvements. Although there were some significant local changes during the eighteenth century, the 'old-style farming' was everywhere prevalent until the nineteenth century. For example, by the year 1800 the lands were still largely held in runrig, a land-holding system common in Scotland consisting of scattered and inter-mingled strips, periodically reallocated by members of the community, which created a 'maze-like landscape with a vocabulary of its own'. Runrig ridges were a rather crude attempt to achieve what the more elaborate land drainage techniques that were employed in later years accomplished. Soil drainage, as much as climate, determined the suitability of land for farming. The single-stilt plough, which scarcely scratched the soil surface, was in general usage, while some 45% of Orkney's land, about 108,000 acres, remained in a still undivided commons. Much of this land served as common pasturage for all manner of livestock and a reliable source of flagstones for building (quite crucial given the absence of wood). Local tenants and cottars also customarily stripped its surfaces of surplus turf. These common lands were a valuable resource for local residents of modest means, and their subsequent loss was to be remembered painfully for generations. For many Orcadians they provided the margin that enabled them to survive. As E. P. Thompson astutely observed, these customary and common rights, which existed 'at the interface between law and agrarian practice', may have been '. . . the area most significant for the livelihood of the poor and the marginal people in the village community'.[1]

Most cultivated lands in Orkney were largely confined to strips along the coast. The absence of overland transportation in pre-improvement Orkney is striking. Only a few roads existed to open up the interior of these islands and horse-drawn carts and ox-wagons were seldom seen. During good years, the islands were capable of producing a sizeable surplus of the staple grains, much of which the local lairds disposed of through a lively export market, principally to Norway, Shetland and the Scottish mainland. The two staple cereal crops were oats and bere, the latter a primitive form of barley prevalent in northern Europe. These grains were principally grown for human consumption.

Old-style farming reflected a society that was simultaneously disputatious and cooperative, in which cash was regarded as an occasional bonus, not the base of the system. In general, it could be said that Orkney's pre-improvement agriculture existed on the sunny side of bare subsistence.[2] However, an unrealised agricultural potential underlay this rather primitive picture. Unlike most surrounding regions, Orkney had soils that were capable of yielding abundant harvests. W. P. L. Thomson's description is particularly apt:

> Whereas glaciation in Shetland and the Hebrides eroded ancient hard rocks, leaving only restricted pockets of good soil, the effects of the Ice Age in Orkney had been to smother much of the lower land in deep glacial clays which developed potentially fertile soils.[3]

These sedimentary soils, derived from Old Red Sandstone, when subjected to intensive and systematic sub-soil drainage, offered much promise for improved agriculture. In addition, the warm waters of the Gulf Stream bestowed both a lengthy growing season and relatively few deep winter frosts.

Thus, the rich resources of a relatively favourable climate, fertile soil, and an advantageous geographical position were far from being developed to their potential *under the old-style farming*. Early nineteenth-century observers, who traversed heathery islands punctuated with small patches of cultivated lower ground, with but few enclosures, were quick to comment. Thomson's verbal portrait of the Orcadian countryside is evocative:

> It is an undulating landscape of long unbroken skylines and distant views. Its openness is accentuated by its treelessness, and before Orkney's mid-nineteenth century agricultural revolution, the absence of field boundaries further contributed to the bareness of the countryside.[4]

Orkney, like much of Scotland, was decidedly a landlord-dominated society. The local Orcadian historian Ernest W. Marwick noted that 'In Orkney, economic power was . . . concentrated in the hands of less than a dozen wealthy proprietors, who exercised all of the privileges of a squirearchy'.[5] In 1800 there were only eight estates that claimed a valued rental exceeding £1000, and these properties accounted for about four-fifths of the land in Orkney. At that time there were only 218 individuals who owned land in Orkney, a marked decline from the 686 landowners recorded in the year 1653.[6] In 1872, quite reliable figures indicate that the fifteen largest landowners owned a total of 171,442 acres in the Islands, or some 71.2% per cent of the total.[7] Under these circumstances, leadership in agricultural improvement could only emanate from propertied individuals, whose hold on the countryside remained quite firm until the First World War.

Eighteenth-century Orkney experienced a considerable diversification of its economic base, thanks to the adaptive skills of its landlord class. The lairds improved agriculture along the margins of the old-style farming system, experimenting with southern ways and new-fangled techniques. They planked some fields (consolidating, squaring and standardising the size of the rigs) in ways that greatly simplified land-holding, began to apply lime and marl to the soil, and introduced such new root crops as potatoes and turnips, which could feed both people and livestock during the long seasons of scarcity, winter and spring.[8] These experiments did not prove profitable. Lack of ready access to markets in the south delayed for several decades any systemic changes to Orkney's agricultural resources. Thus, as Marwick noted, the eighteenth century ended with 'a meagre record of improvement. Only the most elementary experiments were being conducted here and there . . . no intrusions into the primitive economy had begun'.[9]

Since the rewards to be derived from farming the land were limited, the lairds were compelled to look elsewhere for profit. One significant area of economic expansion was that of rural industry, or what current academic fashion refers to as proto-industrialisation. Orkney was unusual because for decades these proto-industries dominated the local economy.[10] In both its proto-industrial phase and its later period of agricultural improvement, Orkney strikes us by the intensity of its economic development. Thus, lairds seized the initiative by inducing their tenants to gather kelp from the seashores and burn it in shoreline kilns, a process that produced a pasty-textured alkali-rich substance for sale to glass and soap-making industries in Scotland and England. Although the kelp industry lasted from 1722 until c. 1830, it did not begin to dominate Orkney's economy until 1780. The necessary investment was minimal, and the profits were enormous—at times the lairds' kelp income was three times what they earned from their rents. Tenants' leases ever more frequently contained kelp-making provisions, as well as the more usual demands for the delivery of such staples as oats and bere. By the middle of the eighteenth century, Orkney leases were also to contain clauses demanding the spinning of certain quantities of coarse linen yarn, and after c. 1805 Orcadians were also noted for their skills in straw-plaiting of fashionable women's hats. All of these industrial commodities were destined for the export market and they brought Orkney more deeply into a cash economy. Thus the Orkneys became inextricably impli-

cated in the swiftly-expanding world of merchant capit-
alism and a burgeoning Atlantic economy.

Though Orkney's population remained static during the
latter half of the eighteenth century, it did possess a large
supply of tractable, cheap labour. This resource served as
Orkney's primary attraction for entrepreneurs. During this
same period, Orcadians increasingly turned to the sea,
either to engage in coastal fishing, to join the Hudson's
Bay Company as contract workers in Canada, or to
volunteer for service with the Royal Navy.[11] All of these
economic activities brought far more money into the
Islands' economy than did agriculture. They also led
toward permanent, primarily male, emigration. Thus
Orkney became a society with significantly more female
than male residents. Cash availability and kelp production
promoted subdivision of the land, and, since access to a
farm no longer served as a basis for marriage and family
formation, ultimately induced a steady population increase.

Yet there is little doubt that these ancillary economic
activities acted as an effective bar to agricultural improvement. For example, the Reverend George Barry, in his
1805 book, *The History of Orkney*, was compelled to
observe:

> The other part of the summer for these eighty years past
> [1720–1800] been, for the most part, employed in the
> manufacture of kelp, highly advantageous indeed, not only
> to the proprietors, but to their tenants, and even some
> measure to the people at large; but as it occupies for the
> space of more than two months those hands which the
> ground stands so much in need of, and might have otherwise
> occupied, it may be considered as among the causes that have
> retarded this excellent and useful art [agriculture].[12]

Barry calculated that over 3,000 people in Orkney spent
the months of July and August in the kelping industry
during the year 1800.[13] New-style farming was later to
make more intensive demands on both labour and capital.

During the years 1770–1800, Orkney's economy was
generally strong. However, early in the nineteenth century
the cycle began to reverse itself, and the economy nar-

rowed, but the Orcadians steadily increased their numbers. For example, the demand for Orkney's linen yarn diminished rapidly after 1805; the army garrison that was stationed in Orkney from 1809 until 1815, along with the cash its soldiers spent, was withdrawn following the peace with France; the Hudson's Bay recruiting declined after 1821; kelp-making all but collapsed after 1830 as new, imported, cheaper forms of alkali became available; and the straw-plait hats abruptly lost their market following a change in women's fashion in 1842.[14] Thomson aptly observed, 'Whether they liked it or not, Orcadians were now forced to take farming seriously'.[15] Just as Scotland suffered from a state of economic marginality within Britain, enduring the characteristic vulnerability of what R. J. Morris has described as a 'low-wage and low-wealth economy', Orkney at that time was to occupy a similar position within Scotland.[16]

The obstacles to the agricultural improvement of the Orkneys were numerous and formidable and were firmly embedded within the social fabric. Nor were they to be easily overcome. In 1814, John Shirreff, the local exponent of agricultural reform, was explicit in detailing these obstacles, as well as the potential for improvement. 'There is no country on earth', he observed, 'that suffers less from the extremes of heat and cold than Orkney, nor any in so high a latitude whose climate, on the whole, is so favourable to the production of the necessaries of life.'[17] At the time he wrote, no more than 84,000 acres of Orkney's total acreage of 384,000 were under cultivation. Visualising himself as a promoter of agricultural improvement of Orkney, Shirreff described it as being 'only in the cradle of existence'.[18] He listed thirteen impediments to improvement:

1. The heavy feu-duties payable to Lord Dundas as donatory of the Crown in the Earldom, and as tacksman of the Bishopric lands (a purely medieval survival).
2. Lands lying in common.
3. Want of leases.
4. Want of inclosures.

5. Smallness of farms.
6. Neglect of herding livestock.
7. Inattention to raising succulent food for supporting livestock during winter and spring months.
8. Want of public roads.
9. Want of markets in the islands for sale of farm produce.
10. The preference given to the burning of kelp.
11. Inattention to the collection and preparation of dung.
12. The deficiency of capital stock which prevails with the great body of farmers.
13. The discrepancy and confusion which have taken place among the weights and weighing machines of these islands.[19]

Though he was as eager as Shirreff to avoid criticism of the character and practices of the landlord class, George Barry, in 1805, added to this lamentable list. He included runrig, 'this most absurd intermixture' of land; the lack of soil drainage, which permitted the fields to remain 'drenched and soaked with stagnant water during the whole winter'; the absence of crop rotation; and the use of the single-stilt plough, which 'has not a single quality to recommend it'.[20] Arguing that 'Every action and practice here seems prejudicial to farming', Barry suggested that Orkney abandon the growing of grain crops, since about one crop in five failed, resulting in frequent bouts of destitution, and that in their place the hills be covered with sown grasses, far better suited to this northern climate. He added that the resulting pasture should be 'henceforth applied to the breeding, rearing and fattening of black cattle'. Both authors also condemned the reluctance of tenants to accept the changes introduced by their 'betters'.

The middle years of the nineteenth century witnessed another notable transformation of Orkney's economy, with a dramatic and intensive agricultural modernisation serving as the driving force for change. Orkney is unusual within northern Scotland in this respect, since nothing on this scale of change occurred in Shetland to the north, much of the Scottish mainland just to the south, or in the Hebrides to the west. Less suited to intensive agriculture in general because of soil, topography and geographical position, most of these were to remain lands more or less rooted in the old-style farming system, or else their inhabitants were compelled to turn to the sea for their livelihoods.

It is worthy of note how little of the agricultural improvement in these islands has been subjected to historical scrutiny. W. P. L. Thomson, in commenting on the absence of much good local agricultural history, saw fit to remark that 'the best account of the nineteenth century farming revolution is an unpublished work written in Dutch!'[21]

Agricultural modernisation in Orkney simply could not take the form of improving the old-style, runrig, scattered-strip, grain-growing system. Only an entirely new agriculture that would supplant the old could justify the considerable expense and investment required. Yet change did occur, and it was rapid on some estates. Usually lairds would transform their home farm as an example to their tenants, while the adjacent lands remained rooted in the old system. Some farms would change, but only gradually. The *New Statistical Account*, compiled in 1842, depicted an island community that was still in the early stages of improvement, one in which an uneasy coexistence of the old and the new prevailed.[22] Old-style farming was subsistence agriculture based on growing grains that were not very distanced from the northern limits of their viability, while the core commodity of the new, commercial agriculture was to be beef-cattle, fed on sown grasses, root crops such as turnips and potatoes, cultivated in the outfield, and a considerable investment of labour and capital.[23] These changes would only be profitable if Orcadians could export live beef cattle and other livestock to the harbours of Aberdeen or Leith. However, little sustained progress could be made in this direction prior to the advent of regular steamship service to the mainland, beginning in the year 1836, and expanding steadily thereafter.[24]

Ernest Marwick felt that Orkney landowners were collectively aware early in the 1830s that economic, social and political changes were on the horizon, and that the old runrig system was 'a monstrous encumbrance', but that the passing of the Reform Act of 1832 awakened landlords to the realization that they were 'defending a stronghold of privilege against accumulating odds'. Nonetheless, 'they held on grimly, knowing that when their fortress was at last overthrown it could never be rebuilt'.[25]

Agricultural improvement in Orkney, when achieved, resulted in dramatic change in the islands' landscape. Sown grasses covering the valleys began to march up the hillsides, the lands held in common were slowly and steadily divided and most often attached to existing estates, fields were enclosed by drystone walls (dykes) and brought under cultivation, strips or rigs of land were combined, or planked, into squared compact fields that were regularly ditched and drained, and selectively-bred varieties of cattle became ubiquitous. The prevailing colour of the landscape gradually shifted from brown to green. The years 1842–1866 saw at least a 75% increase in the arable acreage in Orkney, with a continuing expansion underway until 1883, at which point the process abruptly ceased due to the Great Depression that had a chilling effect on so much of the agriculture of Great Britain.[26] Thus, after nearly a century in which Orkney's economy neglected farming and was so heavily proto-industrial, these islands became a model for the successful expansion of commercial agriculture in northern Scotland.

Notes

1 Edward P. Thompson, *Customs in Common: Studies in Traditional Popular Culture* (New York, 1993), pp. 97–101.
2 W. P. L. Thomson, *History of Orkney* (Edinburgh, 1987), pp. 191–201.
3 *Ibid.*, xiv.
4 *Ibid.*, p. 190.
5 Ernest W. Marwick, *Orcadian*, January 14, 1954.
6 *Ibid.*, January 7, 1954.
7 A. C. O'Dell, *The Land of Britain: The Report of the Land Utilisation Survey of Britain. Part 4. Orkney* (London, 1939), p. 3.
8 Thomson, p. 200.
9 Marwick, *Orcadian*, April 22, 1954.

10 Gilbert Schrank, 'Crossroad of the North: Proto-Industrialization in the Orkney Islands, 1730–1840', *The Journal of European Economic History*, Vol. 21, Number 2, 1992, pp. 365–388.

11 William P. L. Thomson, 'Sober and Tractable? The Hudson's Bay Men in their Orkney Context', 1990. Typescript.

   In order to avoid an indiscriminate press into naval service during the wars against France, landlords and the Royal Navy agreed to annual quotas of between 100 and 150 men from these islands. Volunteers were free to claim proffered bounties for their service. I am grateful to Dr. R. P. Fereday for this information.

12 George Barry, *The History of the Orkney Islands* (2nd edition, Kirkwall, 1867), p. 336.

13 *Ibid.*, p. 386.

14 On the Orkney garrison, see R. P. Fereday, 'Does Haughty Gaul Invasion Threat?', *Scottish Local History*. vol. 30, February, 1994 and vol. 31, June, 1994.

15 Thomson. *History of Orkney*, p. 222.

16 R. J. Morris, 'Scotland, 1830–1914: The Making of a Nation within a Nation', in W. Hamish Fraser and R. J. Morris (eds.), *People and Society in Scotland*, Vol. II (Edinburgh, 1990), p. 4.

17 John Shirreff, *General View on the Agriculture of the Orkney Islands with Observations on the Means of their Improvement* (Edinburgh, 1814), p. 19.

18 *Ibid.*, p. 48.

19 *Ibid.*, p. 167.

20 Barry, p. 341.

21 Thomson, *History of Orkney*, p. xiii. Bart Vink, 'De Ontwikkeling van de Agrarische Bedrijfsstructuur in Orkney, 1840–1930.' Unpublished doctoral thesis, Catholic University of Nijmegan, 1983.

22 *New Statistical Account* (Edinburgh 1842).

23 Thomson, p. 205.

24 A. and A. Cormack, *The Days of Orkney Steam* (Kirkwall, 1971).

   Marwick felt that 'bold leadership' in improvement should have come from Lord Dundas, Earl of Orkney, whose estates comprised more than one half of the valuation of the Islands. However, the absentee Lord was not acquainted with Orkney, and the affairs of his estate were in great disorder. Reform regulations emanating from his Edinburgh business manager were mere 'paper policies', largely without effect. Marwick, *Orcadian*, April 22 and 29, 1954.

25 Marwick, *Orcadian*, May 6, 1954.
26 Thomson, p. 226.

Marwick states that during the period 1855–1870, some 57,000 acres of previously uncultivated Orkney land were turned into crops or permanent pasture. Marwick, *Orcadian*, January 7, 1954.

CHAPTER TWO

The Graemeshall Estate

Located in the eastern half of Mainland, the principal island in the archipelago, the Graemeshall estate was characterised by gently rolling hills sloping southward along the shores of Holm Sound and the waters of Scapa Flow. The Graeme family tenure in Orkney was long-standing, George Graham having arrived in 1617 as Bishop of Orkney. His family had begun amassing lands in Holm parish almost immediately and his son-in-law built the House of Meall there in 1626, though the Bishop chose to reside in his mansion house of Skaill in Sandwick parish on the western end of Mainland. In 1655, when Patrick Graham purchased the property surrounding Graemeshall, Holm parish became the family's principal seat. Thus, Patrick is commonly regarded as the first laird of Graemeshall. Unfortunately for family continuity, neither the fifth laird, Patrick Graeme, Sheriff Depute of Orkney (1739–1786), nor his brother, the sixth laird, Admiral Alexander Graeme (1741–1818), elected to marry (nor for that matter did their two sisters). Thus direct family descent abruptly ceased in 1818.

The seventh laird of Graemeshall was a twelve-year-old collateral descendant named Alexander Sutherland (1806–1894), an Anglicised Scot of gentle birth and expensive tastes. Alexander, whose mother had perished in childbirth, had spent his early years in Jamaica where his father, William Sutherland, had managed an estate named Greenwall for absentee Scottish owners.[1] Although, the young laird subsequently assumed the name Alexander Sutherland Graeme, he exercised whatever influence he had over his own properties from afar, visiting the estate no more than three times during his long lifetime.[2] The Graemes had begun the process of physically distancing themselves from their estate even earlier, during the lifetime of the Sheriff, who spent most of his winter months enjoying the comforts of Edinburgh. One brother, William Graeme, had spent a lifetime in profitable service with the East India Company, though he returned home to Edinburgh in 1768 to die. A second brother, Alexander Graeme, chose a career with the Royal Navy, and lost his right arm in action in 1781 during the Battle of Dogger Bank against the Dutch fleet, where-upon he retired on half pay. Alexander was reactivated during the wars of the French Revolution. In 1795, despite his disability, he obtained both the rank of Rear Admiral and the command of HMS *Glory*, a fine ship in the Channel Fleet.[3] In 1801, following the Battle of Copenhagen, he was stationed for some time with Admiral Horatio Nelson at Sheerness at the mouth of the Thames. His presence there was noted by Carola Oman, Nelson's biographer: 'Vice-Admiral Graeme, Commander-in-Chief at the Nore [naval mutiny of 1797], who lived in one of the hulks, was, like himself, short of a right arm. The officer in charge of the military proved to have a wooden leg'.[4] Undoubtedly, given their similar backgrounds and experiences, the men would have become social acquaintances, if not friends. In 1804, Graeme attained the rank of full Admiral. Thus a combination of health and duty prevented the laird from residing in Orkney. He paid at best a total of three or four fleeting visits to his property. His principal residence throughout his life was his stately home in Edinburgh.

The management of the large estate gradually passed into the able hands of two members of the Petrie family who served the Graemes as factors. In 1782 Patrick Graeme formally entrusted the factorship to his industrious clerk, David Petrie, who served with utter loyalty until 1827, when he passed the burden on to his son. David Petrie, Jr. administered Graemeshall estate until 1861 when the trustees relieved him of his duties. He was 73 years old at the time. Thus, for a period of 79 years, the estate was administered by factors who meticulously preserved the bulk of their voluminous correspondence and kept most copies of outgoing letters. The fortuitous survival, in excellent shape, of the Sutherland Graeme papers opens a window onto the historical past and enables us to analyse the decision-making process during the era of agricultural improvement on a single estate. As we shall see, Graemeshall estate, an apt example of this process, is a worthy object of study.

Graemeshall estate, which occupied virtually the entire area of this fertile parish, was one of the larger Orkney properties, though it would be seen as of fair to middling size by the standards of the Scottish mainland. The estate had the advantage of being compact, thus facilitating a systematic policy of improvement. The Rental of the Crop Years 1830/1831 describes an estate divided into seventy-two farms, occupying 13,034 acres, of which 4,767 acres comprised an undivided commons. The property yielded a gross rental that year of £679. The Graemes, in addition, owned considerable valuable and fertile lands in adjacent St. Ola parish, though it is not possible to quantify their precise acreage. However, the 1830/1831 Rental from St. Ola was £106.[5]

The Graeme family lands were quite conveniently situated within the islands, possessing a lengthy shoreline with many good landing places and sheltered anchorages. Graemeshall was only seven miles from the capital burgh of Kirkwall. Although the estate did have its share of moorland, there was little of the rugged and forbidding terrain that challenged agricultural improvement elsewhere in Orkney. For example, the highest point in the parish is not much greater than 250 feet.

Family papers in the Orkney County Archives contain little reference to the improvement of agriculture during the years in which Admiral Alexander Graeme was laird (1786–1818). The Admiral, as absentee landowner, maintained a warm, affable tone in his correspondence with his factor, David Petrie. He frequently expressed his concern for the health and welfare of the entire Petrie family, which was doubtless genuine. For years he arranged for Petrie to receive a weekly newspaper (one of the very few in Orkney at the time), and the two men avidly discussed world affairs via the post. In addition, the laird, in typical Scottish fashion, employed the patronage system to advance the naval careers of two of Petrie's sons, Archibald and Samuel, who distinguished themselves in their own right as naval doctors. David Petrie, always a master of studied deference, was a dutiful, faithful and efficient servant within the limits of the Admiral's expectations of him. The relationship was quite traditional between laird and factor, as it was with the estate's tenant farmers, and an element of benevolent paternalism was pervasive. The exchange of letters between Petrie and Graeme provided no hint that the cake of custom was to be broken.

Perhaps the most striking impression to emerge from a review of this correspondence is the near-total lack of discussion about the state of agriculture in Holm parish, though circumstances often made it clear that the farming system periodically failed, resulting in considerable hardship for all of the inhabitants. In fact, the Admiral directed his questions more to the state of the kelp crop and its prospects than to the affairs of the land. There was good reason for his concern about kelp. In 1803 the Admiral declared that his income from Orkney consisted of £190 derived from rents and £350 from the 42 tons of kelp produced on the estate that year.

Indeed, among the most carefully and consistently maintained records of the estate was a large set of Kelp Books, kept by both Petries, that describe all transactions in that industry between 1779 and 1836. Thanks to the survival of these accounts, it is possible to derive a much clearer picture of the fate of kelp in Graemeshall than it is of agriculture. The books are also clear indicators of the state of social relations in this area of Orkney, and of the fluctuating role of cash in the local economy. For example, among the names of the kelp-workers listed in these books, a larger percentage are women than those recorded as tenants on the lists of rentals. Thus, one can readily conclude that kelping was a less profitable occupation. In addition, the kelpers were in good part a separate population from the tenants. The 1805 estate rental can be readily compared with the 1805–1807 list of kelpers who had received contracts from the laird for particular tracts of shoreline. Of the total of sixteen individuals thus under contract during these years, only three of those listed were tenants on the estate. None was a major tenant. Many kelpers have last names identical to those of tenants, indicating the strong probability of kinship. It is not unlikely that some of the women were widows or daughters of former tenants. The records indicate that each of the contracted kelpers hired workers to assist in the summer's work, though it is not possible from the records to establish total numbers for the estate. However, the methods of payment are precisely recorded and, not surprisingly, most of the payment was in kind, with very little appearing as cash. Each spring the laird supplied large quantities of oatmeal and beremeal to support the contract kelper and her/his workers for the summer. Any surplus belonged to the kelper, to be disposed of as each saw fit. There is no significant alteration in this procedure from 1779 until 1836.[6]

When the Admiral was pressed for estate expenses in 1806, primarily due to the need to spend £620 for the erection of the new manse (and perhaps church), he chose to hire an expert to survey the kelp shores. He made no attempt to modernise farming practices. The tendency to overcut the kelp shores led directly to a long-term trend of declining kelp output, from an average of about 45 tons in the 1790s to 35 tons per year from 1810 until 1818. The Admiral also regularly sought information on the fate of linen-spinning and he directly sponsored and fostered that industry by annually contributing imported lint seeds (from Riga, Russia, or later from the Netherlands) for the tenants to grow.

The Admiral was always an attentive and interested absentee laird, honestly attempting to keep abreast of estate affairs. For example, he regularly received detailed letters from his factor, made the important decisions, interested himself in the lives of his tenants, and replied to Petrie's queries in a knowledgeable and detailed manner. He also subsidised estate expenditures (i.e., building the new manse, which was an estate expense) from his own pocket. Yet there are few lengthy discussions between laird and factor about agricultural affairs, nor is there any discussion at all of improvement.

The prime topic of discussion between these two men was the impenetrably dense and arcane matter of Superior Duties, owed to Lord Dundas as holder of the Earldom estate, and as tacksman of the Bishopric estate. The heritors of these islands were engaged in an intractable dispute over these matters. The modern mind reels when confronted with the complexity of this surviving medieval social artifact, though it is clear that these Duties were a significant drain on estate income until well into the nineteenth century. The laird was irked because he received nothing in return for these expenses. In fact, these Duties represented the only form of surplus wealth extraction from the estate that bypassed his own pocket.[7]

Although the Admiral did make efforts to maximise his kelp and linen profits, he made no attempt to do so from agriculture. For example, on two occasions, 1802 and 1805, David Petrie explicitly recommended to the laird that he raise the rents of his tenants, in line with the other gentlemen in Orkney. Twice the Admiral declined, though his reasoning is not available to us.[8] Graeme did purchase several parcels of land as additions to the estate, but he did so with a view to their value either in marketing kelp or in avoiding disputes with his fellow heritors.[9] Much estate land was planked and squared. This was done, however, in the interests of equity among tenants rather than agricultural efficiency.[10] The Admiral was always eager to receive news from Petrie about the affairs of the tenants: he regularly used his patronage and influence to advance the careers of their sons in the Royal Navy, he was more than willing to permit widows to remain on farms that were much too large for them to manage effectively, and he rejected all discussion of tenant evictions.[11] In sum,

Admiral Graeme practised paternalism in the broadest understanding of the term.

The agricultural productivity on this estate was adequate to support the population during normal years. However, the northerly location of the Orkneys, when combined with inefficient agricultural methods, practically guaranteed periodic crop failures—usually in one year out of four or five.[12] Too much rain, or perhaps an early frost during harvest, led to dearth and hardship. This occurred in Graemeshall in 1795 when the harvest failed and the lint (flax) crop was lost, leading to much distress among the poor in 1796. The crops failed again in 1803, causing acute suffering during the spring and summer months of 1804, though a 'tolerable good oat crop' emerged to end the hardship. Finally, a poor crop in 1807 produced another bad year in 1808, so much so that the 'Gentlemen of the County' issued a circular letter in search of charitable contributions.[13] Petrie noted in a letter to Admiral Graeme in the spring of 1808 that 'the want is beyond anything that was apprehended in the early part of the year'. By August, he lamented that 'people's cash is exhausted in buying seed and meal'.[14] At no point was the issue of rent reduction entertained by either of the correspondents. Thus paternalism had definite limits!

The limitations of the 'Old Style' farming system are far too numerous to discuss in great detail, although they revolve around the pillars of low productivity, chronic poverty and an endless number of disputes. The estate papers contain an exchange of letters illustrative of the last. On June 9, 1806, three tenants, John Laughton, Jeremiah Sinclair (signed with an X) and William Aim sent to David Petrie a petition that began: 'As we are Tenants to Admiral Graeme for whom you are Factor we find it necessary to lay before you a Great Inconvenience which we Labour under in having Corns and Grasses destroyed and potched by Bestial'.[15] The subject of this complaint was the behaviour of John Mowat, parish schoolmaster of Holm, who kept twice as many animals as his land could comfortably support. He refused to either fence them or herd them, permitting them to roam destructively over his neighbours' fields. The petitioners hoped that Petrie would direct Mowat to alter his behaviour. However, on August 4, Petrie passed the matter on to the Presbytery of Kirkwall, who employed the parochial schoolmaster. Upon receiving no reply on this delicate subject, Petrie wrote once again on November 25. In another letter that same month, 'We Heritors, Elders and Heads of Families in the Parish of Holm' addressed an even longer petition to the representatives of the Church. They extended the scope of their complaint to include 'disorder and idleness' and the fact that Mowat 'is very irregular in observing the hours for teaching'. But the principal point of contention was that he kept 'a superfluous number of Cattle, Horses, Sheep and Swine beyond what can be maintained on the produce of the Croft' and that when this fact was brought to his attention, 'he commonly replies in expressions of bold defiance and threats'.[16] The conflict was protracted, lasting at least until 1807, for on August 6 of that year, Petrie, invoking the authority of Admiral Graeme, the wishes of Mowat's neighbours, and appealing to Mowat's sense of neighbourliness, urged him to sell his surplus sheep at the forthcoming Lammas Market. Mowat's immediate response was an absolute denial of impropriety followed by a reference to 'Complaints proceeding from Spite'.[17] The records fall silent following this exchange.

It is interesting that the tenants chose to handle the problem as they did, by appealing to the established authorities for redress, rather than by dealing with Mowat directly on their own, i.e. by crippling or killing his beasts. Mowat could not on his own have been a person of overawing authority or stature, though he was an employee of the Kirk. Perhaps the affair is indicative of deeply ingrained habits of compliance toward traditional authority among tenants. This dispute also highlights one of the essential limitations of the 'Old Style' farming system, i.e. the dependence of all participants on each others' behaviour. The least efficient and most neglectful farmer had it in his power to bring the entire neighbourhood down to his level of inefficiency, rendering improvements either impossible or futile.

The estate papers indicate that David Petrie was aware of the limits of the agricultural system. In 1809, his son, David Petrie, Jr., travelled to the Scottish mainland to become better acquainted with south country farming. While in Edinburgh, he was graciously accommodated by Admiral Graeme. He also had the opportunity to meet frequently with John Shirreff, a leading exponent of improved agriculture, who instructed him in 'the science of farming'.[18] On February 13, in a letter to John Sherriff, his father, in expressing the following sentiments, sounded a note of despair:

> Our only hesitation is that we have no view of turning such knowledge when obtained to any real advantage in this poor northerly climate on small farms without inclosures, without markets or any encouragement in the current state of the County, of which obstacles you are a competent judge having been acquainted with it all when with us.[19]

Clearly, Petrie was resigned to working in an insular, static and low-productivity agricultural system which it was beyond his power to alter in any substantial way.

During Admiral Graeme's lifetime, Petrie dealt directly with his employer, without resorting to a mediator of any kind. It was a traditional and a personal relationship. There are no letters to be found in the archives from professional trustees, accountants, lawyers, land surveyors, etc.

It became apparent upon the Admiral's death that he was a wealthy man. He was well-connected both in British society and the Royal Navy, his family associations with India and Jamaica were long standing, and his opportunities to augment his wealth were enormous.[20] Since he left a legacy of over £17,000, there can be no doubt that Graemeshall estate represented but a small portion of the family property.[21]

However, in 1818, with Admiral Graeme's death, the direction of affairs changed suddenly and dramatically on the estate. Since the heir, Alexander Sutherland, was a 12-

year-old minor, ultimate authority was exercised by John Irving, second cousin to the admiral, a lawyer and professional manager of estates, who was resident in Edinburgh. Petrie remained as factor, but he was now under Irving's authority.

During the years 1818–1827 all was in limbo at Graemeshall. John Irving in Edinburgh, as the principal trustee of the estate and *curator bonis* of the heir, was the ultimate source of authority, and it was a function he fulfilled with great enthusiasm. But he could grant no new leases that would extend in time beyond the coming of age of the young laird. Nor could he sanction any expenditure that resulted in permanent change or improvement on the estate. The change in tone in the estate correspondence could be felt as though a balmy southerly breeze had been followed by a chilling Arctic gale. A steady dose of cold economic rationality emanating from Edinburgh was accompanied by a frigid style of writing devoid of warmth or sentiment. Irving's letters to the Petries, father and son, from 1818 until his own death in 1850, reveal little about him as a person. The only emotion ever evident is a chiding impatience with the human foibles of others. There is no doubt that Irving felt only contempt for the manner in which the estate had been run, for the way the books had been kept, the indulgences that had been routinely granted to tenants, the level of rents collected, and the management techniques of the factor. Any practices reflecting custom, tradition, or circumstances unique to an island community were unworthy of serious consideration.

This impersonal mood was evident in the very first letter sent to Petrie by Irving. Petrie received a note (a mere three lines) from Irving, penned on August 5, 1818, informing him of the Admiral's death in Edinburgh following an illness of several months.[22] On August 18, a somewhat longer letter tersely requested an inventory of all moveable property, as well as an exact account of all rents, arrears, and debts on the estate. On August 21, Irving dispatched an additional letter demanding an 'exact account' of the first half of 1818. Irving acknowledged, on September 17,

Petrie's response of September 9, but he sternly reprimanded the factor for having 'misunderstood the nature of
the Account of the late Admiral's funds required'. The
letter concluded with further instructions on how to
'render a correct Account.[23] This first exchange is all too
typical of the impatience, denigration, and didactic tone
evident during much of the next 32 years. All of these
demands were without precedent on the estate and were
undoubtedly unsettling to Petrie who had been factor for
36 years, to the expressed satisfaction of his former lairds.
They also reflected the cultural chasm that divided these
two men.

The stream of instructions was quite relentless. In 1819,
Irving observed that the rentals in Graemeshall 'do not
appear to vary from year to year', that the collection of
rents and fees was all too frequently delayed for a year or
more, that the records of income from a variety of sources
were all kept in a common account, rendering the estate
finances impenetrable to the eyes of auditors, and that no
tenant had ever been removed for non-payment.[24] Irving
inquired about practices on other Orkney estates and noted
that 'a considerable indulgence is always given' about rent
collection in the Islands, but that Graemeshall was singular
when it came to leniency: 'To allow two full rents to be
owing at one time must be very bad management everywhere in my opinion'. Irving was precise in his remedy: 'I
am clear . . . that the rents must be paid in full during the
autumn following, that is in October, 1819 for Crop 1818
at the latest', and distinct accounts must be maintained for
different sources of income.[25] Thus Irving was prepared to
streamline the existing agricultural system, despite all of its
faults, but was not yet ready to attempt to change it. Yet it is
significant that this was the first extended discussion
concerning the subject of agriculture contained in the
estate correspondence.

Unfortunately, none of Petrie's letters from 1818–1820
survives, so we are unable to read the factor's response to
such chiding as 'the mistakes you have made . . .'.
However, in 1822, in a letter to his son Samuel, a

Naval doctor, Petrie shared his deep concern about Irving's suggestions:

> He thinks the Tennants ought to pay their Rents at an earlier period each year than they do, but it is not easy for them to scrape it together in these dull times when their articles will not sell, and it is now perfectly known that this Country is drained of Cash and little way to get any in.[26]

And again, one year later, Petrie shared his concern for the tenants: 'I am just now settling with the Tennants for Crop 1822, Money very scarce, *no* Cattle sales . . . the Cattle used to be the best Feather in my Wing – now it is cut short'.[27]

In the midst of the economic downturn, and the unaccustomed chores, burdens, and criticisms to which Petrie was subjected, it is only natural that he feared for his family's future. In 1824, at the age of 71, as he awaited the first official audit of his accounts by a professional accountant in Edinburgh, Petrie expressed concern in another letter to Samuel: 'I could have wished to have had all these settled so as I might have known more perfectly what ground I stand upon. It must however be waited for. It is a great struggle to obtain clear payments from the Tennants . . .'[28]

In the midst of these administrative changes, John Irving began to look beyond mere improvements of an antiquated agricultural system. In two letters he wrote in 1821 to David Petrie, he began to outline an ambitious scheme for the improvement of the estate, on a scale and model more typical of the Scottish mainland than of Orkney. In conception and inspiration, the vision drew nothing at all from local experience or circumstances. The trustee had never set foot in Orkney, where such large-scale improvements were as yet unknown. Though rich in detail, Irving's suggestion are easily reduced to essentials. On March 14, he observed to Petrie:

> From Everything I can learn as to the Estate of Graemeshall, it seems clear that a very great improvement might be made on it by allotting the farms differently, inclosing and granting

leases. The lands, I have been told, are generally possessed in small detached pieces lying interspersed [runrig] and the sheep have not been confined to the higher grounds [absence of enclosure], no turnips or sown grasses can be preserved in winter . . . I think it desirable to have a better allotment in view to prepare for this [a permanent change when Alexander Sutherland Graeme came of age in 1827]. On this account I would wish to have a Plan of the Estate as at present occupied and a measurement of it distinguishing arable from the grass lands and the meadow or green pasture from the muirlands and mosses.

Irving proceeded to indicate that he foresaw a prosperous future for the estate specialising in livestock production, not in grain. Finally, Irving indicated that he would like to have the estate professionally surveyed.[29]

In October, 1821, Irving pursued this subject further, but, as usual, the letter began and ended with matters purely business:

There are three different plans which might be adopted in order to have the sheep and cattle which are grazed on the hill ground prevented from injuring the arable lands and green crops grown on them—the 1st by setting the hill ground as a grazing farm.

He suggested that hiring shepherds from the south of Scotland would insure that the system would work and would yield a far greater profit, since a smaller number of sheep of an improved breed would yield more meat and wool. Irving denigrated Orkney as a bothersome anachronism, noting that 'The management followed in Orkney was general in the south of Scotland a century ago . . .' He continued: 'The second plan is to inclose the hill ground by a march dyke so as to separate it from the arable land'. He advocated a five-foot-high drystone dyke, which he estimated would cost from £100–£150 per mile. The tenants would defray the costs by paying increased rents. Finally,

The 3rd plan is by obliging the proprietor of the sheep and cattle to herd them. This can be easily accomplished. They are bound to do so by law and it is only necessary to enforce the Act of 1686. The sheep, horses or cattle may be detained every time they are found till this penalty is paid . . .

Irving urged that the final plan be immediately adopted, and that printed notices be posted throughout the estate warning tenants and subtenants of their liability.

Toward the letter's end, Irving got to the heart of the matter: 'As long as the hill pasture is occupied as a Common, there will be no great improvement on the stock of sheep, cattle, etc. in the Parish, no draining of any part of the grazing ground or amelioration of the pasture'.[30] It is clear that in 1821 Irving envisaged the estate's future as a livestock-producing venture, with enclosed fields, extensively ditched and drained, and a divided commons. Sown grasses, for use as livestock fodder, would replace in large part the traditional staple grains of oats and bere. Finally, private property rights would triumph, vanquishing all usage and property claims based on community rights and custom.

There were some significant circumstances that Irving neglected to consider, i.e. the lack of ready access to southern markets, the multiplicity of small, frequently uneconomic farms, the absence of a local coercive tradition that would permit effective enforcement of his changes, and the fact that no local model was present for those implementing the changes to emulate. Nor is there any indication that Irving made any attempt to assess the financial costs associated with such an undertaking. Undoubtedly one of the reasons for the future difficulties was that a modernisation scheme appropriate for the Lothians was to be implemented in Graemeshall estate.

For the most part, Petrie endured this barrage of changes, along with the sharp questioning of his management practices, with great stoicism. He drew strength from his deep religious faith and a sense of duty and obligation that was fundamental to all that he did.

One persistent source of concern, however, was his ignorance about the young man who had inherited the estate in 1818, Alexander Sutherland Graeme. In a letter to

his son, Samuel, in 1823 Petrie bristled with curiosity: 'I
believe the Young Laird of Graemeshall has been all
Winter at the Classes [in Edinburgh University]. Have
you seen him or do you know anything of his character?'[31]
Three years later, Petrie began to receive answers to this
question, but they would scarcely have pleased him. In
May, 1826, his son Archibald observed:

> I have not seen the young Laird. . . . You heard as to the party
> he gave at Oman's [hotel] where he is living. I hear it cost
> £600 but I can scarcely believe it cost as much . . . A
> considerable quantity of champagne [was] on the boards
> . . . he wants to make a considerable hole in his property.
> I think he will soon be ruined.[32]

On June 29 of the same year, an elderly family friend in
Edinburgh, Miss G. Traill, reinforced this image of the
laird, describing him as

> a vain, selfish, extravagant and foolish lad with neither honour
> nor principals. . . . I am extremely sorry for his father's family,
> as well as for the Admiral's sake that he is what he is. He takes
> all from his mother's family, nothing of his father's.

In November, Miss Traill added to this picture by noting
that the young laird 'made a great fool of himself here—I
am truly grieved he is so poor a representative of the
worthy family he has succeeded. . . . It was a pity the
Admiral had not lived a while longer to have seen and
known something about him'. Her final contribution to
this portrayal of the 21-year-old was in 1827: 'he is a dirty
poor looking man in his appearance, yet as proud as old
Nick'.[33] As we shall see, the laird's character, particularly
his penchant for dispensing with large sums of money, were
to affect decisively the fortunes of the estate during the
years of improvement.

By far the most important of the elder Petrie's concerns
during his declining years was the fate of the one son,
David, Jr. (1788–1869), who chose not to seek a career in
the larger world, preferring to remain at home and care for
his parents. He was a serious and diligent young man, of an
exceedingly pious bent. His father worried deeply about

him, repeatedly soliciting his more successful and worldly brothers to provide for his care in the future if it proved necessary. The elder Petrie made numerous inquiries among the notables in Orkney about a position for his son, either as an estate factor, Crown official, or farmer. In the 1820s young David tried and failed to earn a living in the herring fishery, but his primary interests at that time were religious, particularly in the fate of the growing Secession Church in Orkney in which he was deeply involved. In 1825, David, Senior, openly despaired: 'Owing to his abiding hitherto with me he has not had it in his power to do much for himself in a pecuniary point of view.'[34] Good fortune did finally prevail, however, when the estate trustees agreed to appoint David, Jr., as successor to his father as factor on the Estate of Graemeshall. He began his duties following the harvest in the autumn of 1827.

David Petrie, Sr., submitted his final account for Crop year 1827, which is when the improvement of the estate began to be implemented. The total income for the estate for that year, including funds from rentals, teinds, multure sold, and from the sale of kelp (£183), amounted to £765. Expenditures in this pre-improvement account were minimal, and Petrie was able to remit over £180 to the care of John Irving in Edinburgh. There was no mention in the Account of arrears of rents by standing tenants, nor did the ledger convey any sense of distress or crisis in the estate's affairs. However, a very different picture would gradually emerge as improvements progressed.[35]

The year 1827 saw a convergence of several events on the estate of Graemeshall. These included the coming of age of the laird, which allowed for the making of permanent decisions for the first time in nearly a decade; the appointment of the young David Petrie, Jr., to the position of factor; unmistakable signs that the kelp trade, which had permitted such easy infusions of cash into the Orkney economy, was nearing an end; and the decision to commence improvements on a large scale, over a short period of time.

There is no doubt that John Irving initiated the move

toward improvement, but it is equally certain that the laird and the factor of the estate wholeheartedly embraced this crucial decision. Nonetheless, as an externally-conceived idea, it was based on experiences and circumstances more common to the mainland of Scotland than to an island named Mainland in the Orkneys. Thus, it was imitative to the core. For example, before reliable and regularly-scheduled steamships were available, no local agricultural improver resident in Orkney ever proposed the sudden transformation of an entire estate, investing a sum double the rental on improvements, over a timespan of about five years, employing the skills of sitting tenants, without investigating the marketability of a new product (live beef cattle and sheep). It is evident from the estate correspondence that for John Irving, improvement was a *magnum bonum*, an end in itself, an article of faith. It is astonishing that a mind that was so exacting and calculating in all matters at no time made written reference to the vital question of how large numbers of livestock would be transported across the Pentland Firth to Caithness, or through the North Sea to the ports of Aberdeen or Leith. The other estates Irving managed, in and near the Lothians, evidently did not face such a problem. Irving displayed similar naivety in his assumption that the extensive common lands would be equitably divided among the proprietors by 1831 at the latest, when, in fact, the process was only to begin in 1844. Thus, enormous expenditures were undertaken, but they rested on the flimsiest of assumptions. An improved Graemeshall estate was to escape the hands of its creditors by only the narrowest of margins.

In November, 1827, David Petrie, Jr., requested guidelines on estate management from Samuel Laing of Papdale, heritor, neighbour, improver, and family friend. Central to Laing's advice was the basic premise: 'The first object and leading principle in the management of an Estate ought to be—to lay out nothing—and to draw in as much as can be fairly and judiciously done by increase in the Rental'. Laing followed this with instructions to improve the poor roads on the estate, but only by employing 'statute labour of the Parish . . . with no expense to the Proprietor'. Laing also made reference to a reordering of the land:

> A new arrangement of the Land is . . . absolutely necessary. I would recommend that without delay a distinct portion of land contiguous to each [farm] should be perambulated along with the tenant without any regard to the Riggs he may at present hold in inconvenient and distant situations and the portion to him a fair rent from next Martinmas: if no agreement can be made I would recommend issuing the usual warnings and letting the farm at the following Martinmas to the best bidder.[36]

When the young laird came of age in 1827, he promptly stated his intention to play an active role in the management of the affairs of his estate. Without delay, and practically unannounced, in October of that year, he paid his first visit to his property. For eight days he stayed with two friends in a Kirkwall tavern, but he visited Graemeshall for only three days. Nonetheless, he did busy himself with learning the routines of farming in these northern lands.[37] He retained fond memories of this visit and looked to Petrie for instruction in matters of improvement for several more years, until the time arrived when his interest in his estate did not extend much beyond the subject of money. Shortly after Graeme's visit, plans were put in motion to hire the Edinburgh land surveyors, the noted firm of Miller and Grainger, as a preliminary step toward improvement. They carried out their work during 1828, and the results arrived in the hands of Petrie and Irving by April, 1829. Two wall-size, multi-colored original survey maps of the estate are currently on deposit in the Orkney County Archives.[38]

Notes

1 Personal interview with Alison Sutherland Graeme, Bethea Warthew and Sheena Wenham, St. Mary's, Orkney, June 24, 1993; *The Orkney Herald*, December 12, 1894, 'The Late Mr. Sutherland Graeme', p. 5.

2 Patrick Neale Sutherland Graeme, *'Pateas Amicis': The Story of the House of Graemeshall in Orkney* (Kirkwall, 1936), pp. 44–51.

3 Patrick Neale Sutherland Graeme, *Orkney and the Last Great War: Being Excerpts from the Correspondence of Admiral Alexander Graeme of Graemeshall, 1788–1815* (Kirkwall, 1915), pp. 5–6.

4 Carola Oman, *Nelson* (London, 1967), p. 413.

5 Orkney County Archives (OCA), Sutherland Graeme Papers, D5/33/13. I have retained the original spelling throughout.

6 Ibid., D5/11/5, D5/39/5. Alun Howkins, in *Reshaping Rural England: A Social History, 1850–1925* (London, 1991), p. 20, has recently described similar methods of payment in kind, particularly in some of the remoter areas of England (Northumberland), generally among the shepherd population.

7 John Shirreff offers the best (and quite lengthy) discussion of this topic in all of its agonising complexity, and explains how it had impeded the pre-improvement economy of the Orkneys: Shirreff, pp. 168–174.

It is not at all clear from surviving records whether the Graemes bought out their feu-duties, as did the Balfours in 1843.

8 OCA, ibid., D5/8/3 and D5/8/6.

9 Ibid., D5/8/6.

10 Ibid.

11 Ibid., D5/8/1–D5/8/18.

12 Ernest W. Marwick described it as 'a life absurdly open to calamity', with 'savage enemies constantly lying in wait— hunger and disease'. Marwick, *Orcadian*, February 11, 1954.

13 OCA, ibid., D5/39/5.

14 Ibid., D5/8/9.

15 Ibid., D5/8/7.

16 Ibid.

17 Ibid., D5/8/8

18 P. N. Sutherland Graeme, *Orkney and the Last Great War*, p. 54.

19 OCA, D5/8/10.

20 Sutherland Graeme, *Orkney and the Last Great War*, pp. 5–6.

21 The Admiral's Deed of Legacies (filed in 1813) provides for 24 cash bequests, including £1000 each to 'John Irving WS, Alexander Irving Adv, and Wm. Irving'. He also granted £500 to 'David Pettrie Factor'. Though the 'Poor of Holm' were recipients of the sum of £100, Alexander Sutherland, heir to the Orkney estate, received nothing: OCA, D5/8/18.

22 *The Scotsman*, August 15, 1818, included the following an-

nouncement of death: 'At Edinburgh, on the 5th inst. Admiral
Alexander Graeme, of Graemeshall'.

23 OCA, Ibid., D5/8/18.
24 Ibid., D5/8/19.
25 Ibid.
26 Ibid., D5/9/4.
27 Ibid., D5/9/5.
28 Ibid., D5/9/6.
29 Ibid., D5/9/3.
30 Ibid.
31 Ibid., D5/9/5.
32 Ibid., D5/10/1.
33 Ibid., D5/10/2.
34 Ibid., D5/9/7. David Petrie, Jr., was offered a lucrative career
   opportunity outside Orkney. In 1830, his enterprising brother
   Archibald, a naval doctor, sought to induce David to emigrate
   to Quebec and share in the farming of some of the 800 acres of
   land he owned there. He also informed David that he had been
   named his heir in his 1824 will. Evidently David declined the
   offer to emigrate. Their brother Samuel died at Graemeshall in
   1828 of illness he contracted during service as a naval doctor in
   the tropics. He was only 27 years old: P. N. Sutherland Graeme,
   The Orkney Herald, May 6, 1952. D5/3/6.
35 Ibid., D5/12/6.
36 Ibid., D5/10/2.
37 Ibid., D5/10/2; '*Pateas Amicis*': *The Story of the House of
   Graemeshall in Orkney* (Kirkwall, 1936), p. 44.
38 OCA D5/10/3. For a fine and helpful discussion of the
   singular importance and professionalization of the role of
   the land surveyor in the process of improvement, see Susan
   A. Knox, *The Making of the Shetland Landscape* (Edinburgh,
   1985), pp. 94–112.

CHAPTER THREE

The Protagonists: Irving, Petrie
and Sutherland Graeme

There is no doubt that Irving and Petrie were the implementers of the extensive improvements of the estate, but they were supported enthusiastically by the absentee laird, who, throughout his life, tended to reside in a variety of seaside resorts on either side of the English Channel.[1] Graeme was grateful for all of his employees' efforts on his behalf and offered advice whenever asked. The correspondence indicates that Petrie made a sustained effort to educate the laird and, for a while, the young man attempted to respond in a knowing and helpful manner. However, by 1832, when both laird and the estate were independently struggling with crippling debt, Graeme's interests in estate matters notably waned. More and more, he looked to the estate solely as a source of money to extricate himself from the clutches of his numerous creditors.

Since human agency looms so large in this study, a brief description of the three personalities who for years worked with, and even more frequently at cross purposes with each other, is in order. It is evident, from the hundreds of items of correspondence, that each of these three resembles, to a remarkable degree, an ideal type.

John Irving, W. S. (1770–1850), the estate trustee, was the second son of George Irving of Newton (in Lanarkshire) and the younger brother of Alexander Irving, Advocate, who later in life became Lord Newton. As an adult, John was doubtless an individual whose demeanour of stiff, unbending rectitude created a lasting impression. Yet, paradoxically, in his youth Irving was one of Sir Walter Scott's dearest and most constant companions.[2]

As young men Scott and Irving would enjoy long walks together toward places of majestic beauty in and near Edinburgh, such as Arthur's Seat, Salisbury Crags, Blackford Hill or the Braid Hills. Upon reaching their destination, they would read romances of knight errantry and tell each other 'interminable tales filled with battles, giants and enchantments'.[3] Both Scott and Irving remained close throughout their days at Edinburgh University, though their paths in life later diverged. They continued their lengthy rambles through the Scottish countryside, venturing eight to ten miles beyond the city toward some of the abandoned old castles in the surrounding hills, where they would once again pursue their medieval romantic visions. One of Scott's letters in 1795 offers the contemporary reader a fine portrait of the young John Irving:

> Upon the mountains of Tipperary—John with a beard of three inches, united and blended with his shaggy black locks, an ell-wand-looking cane with a gilt head in his hand, and a bundle in a handkerchief over his shoulder, exciting the cupidity of every Irish reparee who passes him, by his resemblance to a Jew pedlar who has sent forward his pack.[4]

The two friends seem to have gone their separate ways following their university days, though their paths did occasionally cross in the small world of the Edinburgh elite. Their last recorded contact was in April, 1830, when Irving paid a two-day visit to Scott's estate of Abbotsford. At that time, Irving's brother, Lord Newton, was arbitrating the renowned case between Scott and the publishing house of Constable, in which Scott's entire personal fortune was at stake.[5]

It is a task that almost defies the imagination to reconcile the image of the young, romantic John Irving with that which appears in the estate correspondence. Irving's professional legal world has been aptly described by Michael Fry: 'In Edinburgh were hundreds of them, members of the Faculty of Advocates or Writers to the Signet, thronging to the central law courts to service the interests of the nobility and the landed gentry . . .'[6]

Intellectually, the adult John Irving was a fine example of Edinburgh Enlightenment rationality, since he appeared to be fully confident in the ability of the human mind (particularly his own) to harness the forces of nature in the interests of progress and prosperity. In short, he was a fervent ideologue. But he evidently also shared much of the blindness and arrogance associated with such rationalist thinking. For decades he worked diligently and ceaselessly on behalf of the estate and of Mr. Graeme, churning out an endless stream of correspondence. At no point did he seem in the least unsure of himself, or without an argument as how to proceed.

Virtually all of Irving's letters evince an almost religious faith in the virtues of improvement, viewed as an end in itself. To his mind, hard work, in combination with meticulous subservience to his prescribed path, would inevitably yield rewards. It is also indisputable that Irving viewed regional customs, practices or economic circumstances as little more than nuisances blocking him from his goals. He scorned them with undisguised contempt. Nor did Irving make any effort to comprehend how an island community could be different from one on the mainland, or how local culture could transform, warp, or subvert efforts that elsewhere might be effective and practical. When caught by an unexpected turn of events, Irving inevitably pushed harder in the same direction. He endlessly reiterated that his rules be followed to the letter, even when it was abundantly clear that none of his approaches was working. He was a man with little sense of place and no feel for people. Therefore, it is not at all possible to see any traits of the romantic youth in the John Irving who appears before us. Though he was unquestionably highly competent, he was nonetheless limited, humourless, irascible and impatient.

David Petrie, Jr., was very much a local product. He even reflected the east Mainland portion of Orkney in which he spent his entire life. He was deeply pious, generous, provincial and rustic, yet he was also plainly a man of great intelligence, wide reading and understanding. However, whenever pushed to be more energetic, or to perform tasks promptly, he demonstrated that he had a sense of timing and efficiency that flowed more with the seasons and the weather than with either the clock or the calendar. Whatever belonged to him belonged also to those who inhabited his world, including family and friends. Petrie displayed genuine skill in implementing improvements on the estate, but he was equally adept at resisting all types of pressures and threats from Irving. The factor earnestly believed in improvement on the estate, but more for the sake of those who lived on it, and in Orkney. A good deal of his time and effort was spent helping neighbours and family to acquire the skills necessary to improve their properties. He roamed widely throughout Orkney, sharing his expertise and experiences, judging cattle contests, offering advice, attending religious services, serving as witness for division of common lands, etc. Throughout his entire adult life, he was a well-known local personality. Most vexing to Irving, and to the trustees who followed him, was Petrie's more than casual attitude toward numbers, whether it was a matter of providing them at all, adding them correctly, or anticipating what they might be. For over three decades, those in authority on the estate found it a chore of the first order to extract from Petrie a precise annual account of the crop.

Petrie remained a lifelong bachelor, seems to have managed his personal affairs quite poorly, and would have died bankrupt and impoverished but for the loyalty and generosity of his laird who permitted him to remain on his farm almost to the end of his life. On the whole, it is difficult to understand Petrie's motivations for the prodigious efforts he expended, as well as for enduring the years of abuse that he was forced to take. Material reward was certainly never a part of it, for the records indicate that he received none, beyond his annual salary of £25. Most probably one would have to look to his strong religious convictions and the habits of deference that were an important pattern in his family's history.

Alexander Sutherland Graeme (1806–1894) is somewhat harder to place. He emerges less clearly from the surviving correspondence, though his behaviour is consistent and clear. He was born in 1806, most likely in Jamaica, where his father, William Sutherland (son of Dr. Hugh Sutherland of Kirkwall), managed the sugar plantation called Greenwall. His mother, Henrietta, daughter of James Fea of Clestrain, Orkney, died in childbirth. Alexander's father died later in the same year, of unknown causes. There is little information about his childhood or who was responsible for his upbringing, though his obituary mentions that his education was superintended by a Rev. Malcolm.[7] Alexander is recorded as attending (but not necessarily graduating from) Edinburgh University. In 1827, at the age of 21, he married a woman of property, Mary Anne, daughter of Robert Graham of Cossington, Somerset, younger son of Graham of Kinross and Member of the Supreme Council of India. They had two children, Alexander Malcolm (1845–1908) and Henrietta Florence (d. 1869).[8] His obituary makes no mention of his three visits to Orkney or the pioneering role of his estate in agricultural improvement. Instead the article is adulatory in its long discussion of Graeme's role as a lifelong enthusiast for the cause of the Conservative Party and as an active member of the Church of England.

From the evidence that is available about this family, it is apparent that its behaviour conformed to a larger, characteristically Scottish, pattern. Not only had the Graemes been gradually separating themselves from Orkney ever since the eighteenth century, but several family members were seeking career and fortune within the wider expanse of the Empire or in the Royal Navy, i.e. William Graeme in India, Admiral Alexander Graeme in the Navy, William Sutherland in Jamaica and Robert Graham in India. In addition, the family was assuming an identity that was simultaneously less Scottish and more British.[9] Furthermore, several family members' lives follow the pattern recently described by Alan Karras, who noted that many Scots, making excellent use of their superb professional education, and reacting to the rather restricted career opportunities at home, chose to reside abroad in warmer colonial climes in the temporary pursuit of a quick fortune. These Scots had no intention of becoming permanent residents in these tropical colonies. Instead, Karras aptly describes them as 'Sojourners in the Sun'.[10]

As a person, Alexander Sutherland Graeme was evidently warm, generous and always eager to please. However, evidence suggests that he was seldom in touch with the consequences of his own actions. His letters display a strong desire to belong to a community or a place, but apparently he never did. He was the product of a rootless, monied gentry class whose status and prestige were tied to a piece of rural real estate. The laird's lifestyle and his spending had no obvious connection to his income. Thus he was soon head over heels in debt and typically in need of emergency cash. Much of his income was provided by an obviously lucrative marriage contract in 1827.[11] The estate papers make it clear that Graemeshall was of prime importance to him his entire life, though he visited it on only three occasions: 1827, 1832 and finally in 1877. Initially he made sincere efforts to become an involved absentee laird, as the Admiral had been. Making use of Petrie's proffered advice, and Irving's attempts to involve him in estate matters, the laird strived to fulfill his prescribed role. The high point of his enthusiasm was reached in 1832, when Graeme announced his 'desire to make myself useful as a country gentleman', that he planned to move with his wife to Orkney (for the summer months), and perhaps stand for Parliament. Disaster followed quickly. His wife despised her single three-month-long visit to the Islands in 1832. The family ran up enormous unpaid debts while in Orkney, quite possibly by excessive gambling, for which the estate was ultimately responsible, and the storm-tossed return voyage proved to be nearly calamitous. Mrs. Sutherland Graeme refused to visit Orkney ever again, and the laird returned only once more, shortly after becoming a widower. After 1832, his correspondence with Petrie and Irving is ever more limited to the laird's perpetual requests for money. However, Graeme maintained a strong affection for both Petrie and Irving, whom he regarded as benefactors labouring on his behalf, and for years thereafter he provided help for them in any way he could.

Thus the pattern of improvement of the Graemeshall estate was partially the product of the interaction of representatives of three different worlds, i.e. the modern professional estate manager eager to maximise profit above all else, a member of a rural island culture with extensive ties to the local community, and an absentee Anglicised gentleman proprietor. On no occasion did all three of these men meet together. They confined all of their contact to the medium of the Royal Mail. Though all three consistently worked at cross-purposes with each other, they did ultimately succeed in realising the transition from one agricultural system to another.

Notes

1 OCA, D5/10/2.
2 H. J. C. Grierson (ed.), *The Letters of Sir Walter Scott* (London, 1832), Vol. 1, p. 26.
3 Edgar Johnson, *Sir Walter Scott, the Great Unknown* (New York, 1970), p. 48.
4 *Letters of Sir Walter Scott*, Vol. 1, p. 41. Irving, whose nickname among his companions was 'crab', was at that time walking in Ireland with Adam Ferguson, Junior.
5 *Ibid.*, Vol. 2, p. 325 and Vol. 10, p. 263.
6 Michael Fry, *Patronage and Principle: a Political History of Modern Scotland* (Aberdeen, 1987), p. 9.
7 No local obituary of the laird appeared in either Orkney newspaper. However, *The Orkney Herald* reprinted, six days later, an obituary that had earlier appeared in *The Hastings and St. Leonards Advertiser* of December 6, 1894. There is only scant mention of his Orkney estate in the obituary. He was evidently a more significant presence in St. Leonards than in Orkney.
8 *Burke's The Landed Gentry* (London 1898), pp. 612–13.

9 As described in Linda Colley's *Britons: Forging the Nation, 1707–1837* (New Haven, 1992).

10 Alan L. Karras, *Sojourners in the Sun: Scottish Migrants in Jamaica and the Chesapeake, 1740–1800* (Ithaca, 1992).

11 Sutherland Graeme, *Pateas Amicis*, p. 44.

CHAPTER FOUR

Implementation

Neither the techniques nor the technology used to improve the Graeme properties were in themselves uncommon. Rather, they were quite typical of those employed throughout a good part of the north of Scotland. Uniqueness lay in the scale, the scope and the timing of these developments within the islands, as well as the plethorä of unpredictable elements that managed to intrude. The old system of farming was phased out and a new one was gradually introduced. The landscape had to be reordered and the land re-allocated, from scattered strips into squared lots, in accordance with the stipulations of the survey. The fields were fenced and dyked, and the livestock, herded or enclosed in fields, were effectively separated from the ripening crops. The root crops undertook their typical journey from the gardens to the outfields, and extensive subsoil drainage was promoted everywhere. In general, the tenants were encouraged to purchase, at some considerable expense, the new-style tile drains that required little maintenance. Furthermore, the estate had to build and maintain new roads and bridges, constructed for the most part by statute labour, leading toward the wastelands (described as breaklands, muirs, mosses, etc. in the correspondence) that were, for the first time, being brought under the plough. Larger numbers of animals could then be raised for export, with huge quantities of fodder and root crops on hand for keeping stock alive during the long winter months.

For 'New Style' farming to work, several types of arrangement needed to be rigidly enforced, i.e. crop rotation, selective livestock breeding, regular manuring, maintenance of dykes, application of lime, and employment of new cultivation techniques. Thus estate managers found it necessary to move into unprecedented areas of social control, as the surviving written leases demonstrate. Thus inroads into the daily lives of the tenants from above were more invasive than they had ever been. Tenants had to be induced to abandon traditional husbandry practices, in exchange for the promise that they would realise gains in the future. They were also offered the new protection of printed long-term leases. Threats that were unheard of in the days of paternalism, such as removal for non-payment, were now quite routine, though they were seldom enforced. Some people who had no role in this larger scheme, such as sub-tenants and cottars, after an initial period in which their labour was required, eventually found themselves with no secure position on the estate. An improved estate could usually operate with much less labour than one employing pre-modern methods. Petrie and Irving thus had to make full use of all the powers they possessed, both persuasive and coercive, in order to bring this new system into being and to have it work properly.

To put matters in perspective, it is important to clarify how unprecedentedly early these improvement efforts were in the case of Graemeshall. Though all other Orkney estates currently lack detailed studies of their improvement experiences, the secondary literature contains numerous examples that demonstrate that the other Orcadian improving landlords began the process much later (typically during the late 1840s and 1850s). The *New Statistical Account*, compiled for Orkney in 1842, generally depicts an island in only the early stages of improvement. In some parishes, parish ministers report virtually no modernisation. For example, in the parishes of Firth and Stenness on western Mainland, the Reverend William Malcolm remarked that 'the improvements in this parish, for many years, have been very trifling'.[1] Other ministers were equally despairing. The Reverend Walter Traill, of the parish of Lady on the island of Sanday, wondered: '. . . for what individual, removed a single step from sanity, will risk his capital on improvements from which he has no certainty of profits'.[2] Even more telling were the remarks of the Reverend James Smellie of the parish of St. Andrews, adjacent to the parish of Holm: 'Improvements of any kind in agriculture cannot be said to have yet generally commenced. One is animated by the anticipation, rather than by the appearance of its first dawn'.[3] In similar vein, the Reverend William Grant of the parishes of Cross and Burness, again on the island of Sanday, would have liked to have witnessed the sale of the land to 'hard-working sure-going men, with sufficient capital, and with common sense enough to make their plans conform to soil, climate, and circumstances: in fact, just such characters as are usually described to be the most suitable for emigrating to the colonies'.[4] Nonetheless, several parish ministers were able to report significant agricultural improvement in various parts of Orkney. Generally, the scale was rather small, i.e. hundreds of acres at most, in contrast to the thousands in the case of Graemeshall (2,850 improved acres, as reported by the Reverend Andrew Smith in 1842).[5]

The other noteworthy improving lairds thus began their work at least a decade after Graemeshall's pioneering efforts. Consequently, they were well able to take advantage of government drainage and roadbuilding loans, not to mention a regularly-scheduled steamship service to the south.[6] For example, in 1845, Archer Fortescue, a Devonshire gentleman, purchased the 3,000-acre estate of Swanbister in north-west Mainland. Although the lands were virtually unimproved at the time of purchase (the total value of all crop and stock in 1845 was a mere £81), Fortescue brought to bear several decades of effort, considerable capital expenditure, and ruthless social management. By 1872, the value of crop and stock had risen to £4,000.[7]

In a similar vein, the Balfour family's properties on the island of Shapinsay were considered worthless wasteland, except for the experimental improvements around Cliffdale and the village of Elwick built by Thomas Balfour during the eighteenth century. Yet in 1846, Colonel

David Balfour initiated large-scale reclamation and improvement schemes which radically transformed most of
the island. Although the process was complex and
lengthy, the results were by any measure impressive. In
1848, some 700 acres were arable or under rough grass.
By 1866, the number had increased to 2,031 acres. The
estate was also quite renowned for experimentation in
several areas, i.e. improved livestock, new crops, etc.
Initially the tenants' rents were maintained at a low
level. However, the tenants were also required to erect
new farm steadings at their own expense, and according
to Balfour's plans.[8] All of these improving efforts of the
1840s were profitable, because of rising agricultural prices,
regular, reliable steam transport and the increased value of
Orkney's exports.

The actual record of improvements in Graemeshall, as
reflected in the estate papers deposited in the Orkney
County Archives, provides a picture in which the unexpected triumphed over rational planning. The perils of
implementing this vast scheme, both prematurely and
without proper coordination among the principals involved, became increasingly evident. Many factors in-
truded during the years 1828–1840 that resulted in
almost unmanageable uncertainty:

1. The unanticipated decline of the kelp industry, and the
   loss of income, from 1829 onwards.
2. The agricultural recession of the 1830s and the resulting
   arrears of rent.
3. Indebtedness of Alexander Sutherland Graeme.
4. Delay in the division of the common lands in Holm
   parish.
5. Incessant conflict between trustee and factor.
6. Greater than anticipated expenses in implementing improvement.
7. Resistance of tenants to improvement.

Underlying many of these factors was the more general
difficulty of transporting livestock to southern markets
when the sailing sloop was the only option. The remainder of this chapter is devoted to the interplay of these seven

elements and the resultant impact on the agricultural improvement of Graemeshall.

I. Kelp

There can be little doubt that at the moment he proposed agricultural change, John Irving expected that the sale of processed kelp would continue to yield a substantial share of the total income of the estate. Though not many in Orkney foresaw the drop in prices and the decline of the market for the product, this failure to anticipate a trend would prove quite costly to the estate. Since W. P. L. Thomson has published an excellent monograph on the Orkney kelp industry, an outline of the details should suffice.[9] Though it is true that Holm parish was never as widely reliant on kelp as were some of Orkney's more isolated northern isles, the long shoreline within Scapa Flow and along Holm Sound did deliver great quantities of a most valuable commodity that served to cushion the effects of a slack harvest. Furthermore, since kelp was exported, it could provide ready cash to the estate at a time when most other obligations were still paid in kind. Many sub-tenants and cottars depended on the contract work along the shores for their margin of survival, since few could feed their families from their small plots and their occasional inshore fishing. In addition, the price cycle of kelp often moved in a different direction from that of the estate's agricultural products. The careful maintenance of the kelp books on the estate, from 1779 to 1836, is testimony to the obvious importance of this commodity.

In truth, kelp had been declining in value on the estate during the entire nineteenth century. Though prices for the product were high during the war years, productivity was diminishing. Admiral Graeme was so concerned that he had his shoreline surveyed in 1806 in the vain hope that he could raise output. These efforts were futile. In 1798, for example, 44½ tons of kelp brought in £356, while in the year 1800 some 36 tons yielded £300. The decline became more painful in 1805 when kelp sales produced a profit of only £231. This rate held steady until the end of the first decade.[10] By the 1820s, the free trade policies of the liberal Tories permitted the price of Spanish barilla, kelp's imported rival, to drop steeply, undercutting domestic kelp. Kelp was being driven from its accustomed market. The estate rental of 1827 reflected this. The total rental was £537 (for both the lands in Holm and St. Ola). Kelp sales yielded £183, or 34% of the total amount. A good part of the estate correspondence dealt with this decline and its meaning for the future. For example, in 1829, with the survey of the land completed and improvements well underway, Alexander Sutherland Graeme, then living in Brussels, devised a scheme for selling the estate's kelp within the German Confederation. He forwarded to Petrie a letter from a Rotterdam merchant, whom he had met on his honeymoon, that alluded to this large demand that supposedly only Orkney kelp could supply. Petrie had to explain to the young laird the futility of entering new markets at the moment when there was over-production throughout Scotland, steeply declining prices, and the prospect of barilla driving the kelp trade into extinction.[11]

The kelp produced in 1828 and 1829 could not be readily disposed of. That manufactured in 1828 sat in storage for some time, until finally sold in 1830. Of a gross rental that year of £544, the kelp yielded £174, or some 32% of the total amount. Subsequently the kelp fared even worse. The estate could make no further sales until 1831, when the product seems to have been dumped, for not much above cost, for a sum of £132, or a mere 17% of the total rental that year of £784. As Petrie sadly observed: 'Such is the Fate of the Article which formerly formed the best Part of the Revenues of Orkney Proprietors'.[12]

The timing for the estate could scarcely have been worse. There is no evidence that improvements were undertaken in anticipation of the kelp era ending. This sudden plunge in income aggravated the economic pro-blems the estate faced due to its premature improvements. The loss of kelp, in combination with the assault on the

'Old Style' agricultural system, undermined the economic position of the cottar class on the estate. Except for the sporadically successful herring fishing station established with the founding of the village of St. Mary's on Holm Sound in 1830, the only rural industry remaining for this population was that of straw-plaiting, i.e., the weaving of straw hats then fashionable in British markets. The work was available, primarily for women, until 1842, when a sudden change in fashion brought about its extinction.

2. Agricultural recession

Graemeshall estate was not experiencing an economic crisis when improvements began in 1828 and 1829. All of the correspondents were optimistic, at times even ecstatic, over future prospects for both the landlord and tenants. Surviving records do not provide the statistical precision one might wish for. Nonetheless the factor's accounts (annual rentals), lists of arrears of rents, combined with the information contained within the routine exchange of correspondence, when properly evaluated, provide a reasonably complete picture of the affairs of the estate during the transition years, 1828–1840. In general, the economic trends at Graemeshall paralleled those for Orkney as a whole during this period. With kelp gone, grain prices low, and cattle prices uncertain, the Islands experienced a brutal narrowing of their economic fortunes throughout these years.[13]

The surviving accounts recording estate rentals for 1827–1834, if scrutinised out of context, portray an improving estate in which rent collection was becoming increasingly systematic and routine.[14] A fluctuating but favourable picture emerges when one glances at the rents from both Holm and St. Ola parishes. They evidently steadily increased. The combined annual rentals from both parishes were as follows:

Gross Rental	1827	£539
Gross Rental	1828	£546
Gross Rental	1829	£516

Gross Rental	1830	£795
Gross Rental	1831	£785
Gross Rental	1832	£779
Gross Rental	1833	£778
Gross Rental	1834	£734

However, the reality behind these figures posed severe problems for the estate. For example, in 1833 Petrie included in his account an entirely new and ominous item, a list of 'Arrears of Rents'. In that year the accumulated arrears amounted to £332, an alarming figure. It is entirely probable that these burgeoning arrears would account, in part, for the growth in rentals from 1829 to 1830. Most likely, this growth was illusory. Since Petrie was so dilatory in delivering these accounts, frequently years after they were due, there was little chance that such arrears could be anticipated before they became an emergent reality. However, since the arrears did represent money that the tenants were incapable of paying, they signalled a menacing development, particularly at a time of mounting estate expenditure. In a letter dated September 21, 1835, Petrie informed John Irving that 34 tenants were then in arrears for a total sum of £435. In other words, over one half of the estate's tenants (total tenantry of 64) were in debt for over one half of the gross rental (£707).[15] An even bleaker picture emerged in 1836 when Petrie dispatched to Irving a list of 56 tenants who were then in arrears, for a grand total of £673. By this point, the tenant able to pay rent in full was a valued exception to the rule.

The year 1837 was widely seen as one of destitution for the Highlands and Islands of Scotland. Due to the collapse of kelp, several years of deficient harvests, and the nearly total failure of the harvest of 1836, the region experienced terrible despair. The Scottish landed proprietors held a meeting at Egyptian Hall, Mansion House in London on March 11, 1837, on behalf of the destitute. Thomas Balfour, M.P. for Orkney and Shetland, chaired the Committee.[16] He requested a minimum of £100,000 in contributions from Scottish proprietors to stem the tide of misery. However, on April 10, 1837 John Irving indicated that the estate could contribute no cash to this fund, since the proceeds from the estate at that time yielded no more than the interest on the debt. Irving felt that the estate would be generous if it employed the destitute on the roads and paid them in meal and potatoes. The trustee proceeded to despair that there were 'too many inhabitants on the estate . . . a useless number of poor horses and cattle—ill-fed, scrawny, and the oats sown [are] of miserable quality'.[17] It is ironic that Graemeshall estate found itself committed to agricultural improvement at the precise moment in history when the islands experienced their final subsistence crisis.

The factor's account of 1840 hinted at some improvement since it listed only 37 tenants still in arrears, for a total sum of £415, out of a gross rental that was then £775. Irving expressed less despair than he had earlier. The prevailing feeling was that the economy of Orkney was on the mend. Unfortunately no factor's accounts survive for the rest of the 1840s, but on March 29, 1849 Petrie was sufficiently optimistic to proclaim:

> Mr. Graeme's Estate being now in a very different and advanced State of Improvement and Value since the Lands were laid out in Severalty, and the Tenants having become improving Tenants they have also become more unwilling than ever to give up their Possessions, but notwithstanding of this, the Interest of the Proprietor has now to be attended to.[18]

It is indeed significant that no arrears are mentioned on any of the surviving rentals for subsequent years until the 1880's. All indications are that the tenants did not experience great difficulties meeting their rents until that fateful agricultural downturn.

3. Indebtedness of Alexander Sutherland Graeme

Neither Petrie nor Irving appears to have thought highly of either the abilities or the actions of the absentee laird of the estate, but they were so careful in their comments that only an occasional hint of their disapproval of his behaviour appears in the estate papers. The laird lived a profligate lifestyle in his youth, in which he squandered resources at an unimaginable pace, in geographical locations that Petrie and Irving could only imagine from magazines. However, they laboured dutifully in Graeme's service, and made every effort to include him in the making of the larger decisions.

From the earliest communications of Graeme, Petrie and Irving, it is obvious that the young man was quite enthusiastic about the estate, was eager to learn all he could about improvements and delighted in playing his role as the laird of Graemeshall. As soon as he was of age, in October, 1827, he made a practically unannounced visit to Orkney. Without seeking anyone's advice, Graeme proclaimed to Petrie by post his imminent arrival in the Islands. He remained in Kirkwall for one week of bleak autumn weather, accompanied by his brother-in-law and adviser, Oswald Bloxsome. The records indicate that he visited the estate for only three days.[19] There is no indication that he was particularly impressed by what he observed, but he remained a strong enthusiast about the benefits of improvement. For example, on August 28, 1828, Graeme thanked Petrie for several fine letters informing him of his Orkney lands. He announced his marriage, his new residence in 'Brussels, Kingdom of the Netherlands' and regretted that the whirl of summer social events prevented him from visiting the estate that year. However, he entreated Petrie to 'be sure to write me the particulars as to the Improvement of the Estate', which he trusted would 'become more valuable with time', especially since he had 'such careful People' as Petrie and Irving in his service.

For the next year and a half, Petrie meticulously explained to the young man how the estate worked and about the implementation of improvements (i.e. at least three letters are quite specific concerning how a three-stage improving lease worked). He also made a point of soliciting Graeme's advice concerning each major decision. The laird endeavoured to understand the information, contributed his opinions according to his understanding, and remained an ardent team player for some time. However, in 1829 he was perplexed when he observed that 'it certainly appears strange that so large a tract of land should yield so little'.[20]

The first indication of significant trouble between laird, factor and trustee can be detected in a letter of January 4, 1830 that Graeme sent to Petrie in which he requested an account of the total value of his property, including the yearly value of the crop and the cost of superior duties.[21] Having received no reply, he repeated this request on May 29, and, most ominously, indicated that he intended to borrow £300, listing the estate as collateral, for a period of one year.

As the year 1830 came to an end, an unmistakable tone of impatience crept into the laird's letters to Petrie, and his demands for precise answers were unremitting. For example, on December 22, he wanted to know 'What is the exact amount of the sum paid over by you into Mr. Irving's hands per annum after deducting the expenses?' and 'I wish you write once every month to me'. These requests were doubly motivated, by the young man's need for money and by Petrie's lack of response.

The laird was compelled to wait until January 17, 1831 for a proper answer to his request for an evaluation. The picture presented by Petrie was in no way encouraging, particularly if there was anticipation of regular remittances from the estate. Steadily mounting expenditure on improvement dwarfed the declining kelp proceeds.[22] But by July 28, the laird's needs had escalated, as he announced that he was in need of £500 in order to furnish his new house in St. Leonard's-by-the-Sea in Sussex. He wished to know who in Orkney would lend him such a sum, at 5% per annum. Though he reiterated his need for a remittance from the estate, he was quick to lay blame for all of his difficulties on the movement for free trade and parliamentary reform, both of which he trusted would meet with speedy defeat in London. Estate records indicate that Graeme received no money from his Orkney property for either 1830 or 1831.[23]

What followed was a cascade of ascending indebtedness, in which the laird borrowed great sums of money from a variety of sources, and secured the loans either with life insurance policies, or by encumbering the largest, most improved and most productive farms on the estate. Graeme's requests for money from Petrie were relentless, but he also aimed his requests at Irving in Edinburgh. This indebtedness was an undercurrent in all of the correspondence about the estate and led to much hostility between Petrie and Irving, especially since neither man felt himself able to control the situation. On March 3, 1832 Irving revealed to Petrie that he had personally loaned the laird the large sum of £500, yet by November 2 Graeme importuned Petrie for an additional £300, referring to his 'serious and alarming temporary difficulty which was not a fault of mine'. He added urgency by warning that he might be 'arrested and my property taken from me'.[24] No surviving record provides further insight into the laird's sorry dilemma. Petrie could only reply with another expression of poverty, though he did regretfully inform the laird on June 3, 1833 that a £400 bill still remained unpaid from the visit to Orkney of Graeme, his wife and their entourage during the previous summer of 1832. By August, 1833 Graeme's language grew truly desperate: 'I do not know what will become of me', he pleaded.

In a rare moment of candour, Irving confided his thoughts to Petrie on September 28, 1833:

> I was surprised and vexed to learn lately that Alexander Sutherland Graeme had incurred a debt in Orkney of £1,000 by borrowing money from Mr. [John] Spence, the agent of the Commercial Bank of Kirkwall. I cannot understand how he could need all this money! He is proposing to borrow more money to pay for it and pay a high interest and insure his life also—this is a very injurious way of getting money and if continued will reduce him to beggary very soon.[25]

In addition to borrowing huge sums of money for an elaborate lifestyle, the laird was assigning ever larger portions of the estate's rents as security for these debts.

This occurred in the midst of an economic downturn in
Orkney, at a time of difficulties with the estate's tenants and
against the background of constant bickering between
Petrie and Irving. By this time, Graeme's letters were no
longer concerned with matters of agricultural improvement
or with running the estate. The prime topic was money, or
the lack of it.

No improvement in this cycle occurred in the year 1834.
Once again, on June 3, 1834, Irving shared his fears with
Petrie:

> Mr. Graeme has contracted debts in England . . . to the
> amount of £2,500 and wishes money borrowed to pay this.
> He will soon have no income whatever from his lands in
> Orkney. It would require lands yielding a rental of at least
> £200 to be conveyed as a security. But the difficulty is that the
> Superior Duties and minister's stipend are all preferable
> burdens on the rents.

Irving, plainly astonished, felt that under such woeful
circumstances, few would wish to lend.[26]

An important document found in the estate papers sheds
extra light on the laird's now chronic indebtedness. It is in the
form of a lengthy, carefully drafted legal paper, dated March,
1860, entitled 'Memorandum Respecting the Graemeshall
Trust', and contains an outline of the estate's and family's
financial plight, along with a good portion of its subsequent
history. It provides a reasonably clear picture of the manner
in which these potentially ruinous debts were handled and
the family fortune was preserved. In August, 1834 the entire
estate of Graemeshall and all financial obligations connected
with it were consigned to the Graemeshall Trust, with John
Irving having full power of attorney and administrative
authority. All of the personal debts of the laird were held
in security by John Donaldson, Esq. of Broughtonhall, and
following his death, by Donaldson's Hospital.[27] This unquestionably represents an effort by those superintending the
family's interests to protect his fortune (or that of his wife)
from unrestrained profligacy. Existing records shed no
further light on the details.

1. Alexander Sutherland Graeme, 1806-1894, 7th Laird of Graemeshall, painted in his twenties. Courtesy of Sheena Wenham.

2. David Petrie, Junior, 1788-1869. Photograph by Edinburgh Photographic Gallery, 1868. Petrie served as factor of Graemeshall and St. Ola, 1827-1861. Courtesy of the Orkney Library.

3. Graemeshall prior to c. 1870, photographer most likely Alexander Malcolm Sutherland Graeme, who demolished it. The oldest parts dated to the 15th century. Courtesy the Orkney Library.

4. The new Graemeshall, c. 1900. Photographer unknown. Courtesy the Orkney Library.

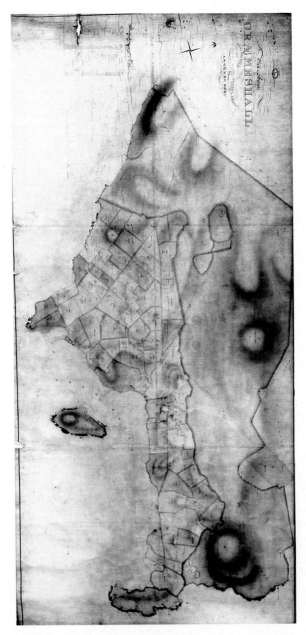

5. Survey map of Graemeshall estate, 1828, Grainger and Miller, Surveyors, Edinburgh. Cultivated lands are confined to the coast; the interior is almost totally commons and wasteland. Courtesy the Orkney Library.

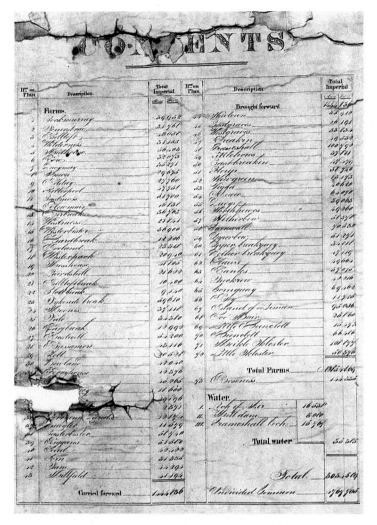

6. Detail from the preceding survey map, the first estate survey in Orkney. It lists 72 farms, giving the name of each: 12,855 acres total. Undivided commons: 4,764 acres. Courtesy the Orkney Library.

7. Single-stilt ploughs, with stone blade, simple to maintain, and capable of being drawn by a single horse or ox. Photographer unknown. Courtesy the Orkney Library.

Ploughing with Oxen (Woman)

8. Woman ploughing with an iron-tipped plough, which gradually superseded the single-stilt plough during the 19th century. Photograph by George Washington Wilson, c. 1890. Courtesy the Orkney Library.

9. Village of St. Mary's, c. 1900, a planned village with fishing crofts, begun 1829, on the Graemeshall estate. Photograph by Tom Kent. Courtesy the Orkney Library.

10. A typical 19th-century Orkney croft, with sod roof and central hearth. Photographer unknown, c. 1890. Courtesy the Orkney Library.

11. Alexander Malcolm Sutherland Graeme, 8th Laird of Graemeshall, at the front door of the old Graemeshall. Courtesy the Orkney Library.

Irving's powers were broad and comprehensive. He had the authority to manage and spend 'without the Consent of the other Trustees in the same Manner as if he had been named sole Trustee'. He was granted four responsibilities: 1. Pay all 'Public and Parish Burdens', including Superior Duties. 2. Settle all debts associated with the property. 3. Pay interest on the personal debts of the laird. 4. Remit to the laird the sum of £200 annually, in four quarterly instalments. These arrangements remained in effect, according to the document, until the death of John Irving in 1850, at which time the executive authority of the Trust passed into the hands of John Scott-Moncrieff and Stuart Neilson. From time to time, Graeme found it necessary to borrow additional funds, but he did so from the trustees, not from the estate, with the sums to be deducted from his marriage contract. Thus, the indebtedness of the laird was being slowly separated from the affairs of his Orkney property. However, given the large figures involved, it is very difficult to imagine that it could have been done without large infusions of capital from some other source. However, the 'Memorandum' remains silent concerning any further details.

The trust agreement now shielded Petrie from too many requests for money from the laird—he no longer dealt with anyone having authority over the estate other than Irving. Thus fewer letters were exchanged between laird and factor, since they had previously had little to discuss other than money. Unfortunately for Graeme, the estate was not sufficiently prosperous for the next several years for his £200 annual stipend to be paid in full. Most years he received nothing. Graeme's complaints about his poverty persisted, and occasionally he would request a loan from the estate. For example, in 1846 he requested from Petrie that he lend him £750, implying that the estate owed him that amount over the years. But the factor had no authority to make such a loan. In September, 1846 the Graemes were compelled to auction off in Bridgewater some 345 personal items, consisting of family furniture, artworks, crystal, etc., for which they realized £256 in cash.[28]

The laird's experience as a perpetual debtor was more than an annoyance and a distracting element to Petrie and Irving. It was a drain on the resources of the estate at precisely the moment when Graemeshall could have used an infusion of capital from the Graeme fortune. Most other improving lairds in Orkney were able to finance similar improvements from family money.

4. Delay in the division of the common lands

In 1800, some 108,000 acres of Orkney's land, or about 40% of the total, still lay in common. At a time when the Islands' proprietors were concentrating on kelp, there was not a great deal of interest in these lands, which lay mostly within the interior of the various islands. Their agricultural potential, though enormous, was not yet apparent. However, as improvements became possible and legislative enactments made division feasible, the Orkney heritors began to view these former wastelands with great interest.

However, between 1830 and 1860, the bulk of the Orkney commons was legally divided in a manner that consigned most of the benefits to the landed class. What is most remarkable is that the division provoked so little contemporary comment.[29] Significant legislation promoting division was passed by Parliament in 1695, but no significant division was achieved in Orkney for 120 years. The barrier to division was the existence of Crown lands in eight of Orkney's parishes, including Holm, that were specifically excluded from the 1695 act. Division required agreement among all of the parish's proprietors. However, an 1829 Parliamentary amendment to the earlier act made division feasible.[30]

In Holm parish, the commons was made up of a large stretch of land, over four miles long and one and a half miles deep, that roughly paralleled Holm Sound and Scapa Bay. These common lands were of vital importance to the local peasant community since they were utilised as pasture to graze and water livestock, to dig and dry peats or to serve as a source of turf and sandstone slabs. From time to time, a few dwellings and huts would encroach upon the commons, surrounded by turf dykes. These were inhabited by squatters, whose legal and economic position was always precarious. The entire commons in Holm consisted of 4,767 acres out of a total parish acreage of 8,457, or 56% of the total.[31] There is little information on the size of the commons in St. Ola parish adjacent to the Graeme property, although these were doubtless extensive. These lands gained renewed importance during the years of improvement as Orcadians again focused on the development of agriculture.

In certain parts of Orkney, the division was a simple, brief and relatively uncontested process. This proved not to be the case in Holm, which was plagued by an agonisingly long conflict among the local élites, leading to extensive delays. At first, Petrie and Irving were hopeful that the task could be completed easily and quickly. In 1827, they expressed concern over the presence of the squatters on the hill ground, especially as this might cause legal ambiguity and delay.[32] However, in the autumn of 1829 Petrie wrote with confidence to the laird of his belief that 'Most likely the Commons will be divided among the Heritors of Holm next Summer' and, he hoped, the Crown would take the lead.[33]

The following year these early hopes began to dim. In August 1830 Irving referred to a dispute 'between the hill ground of Holm and that of the two adjoining Parishes of St. Olla and St. Andrews or Deerness'. By March 4, 1831 Petrie regretted having to inform Graeme that 'the division of the Hills or Moors is . . . as yet unproceeded with'.[34]

Movement toward division accelerated on April 18, 1831 when His Majesty's Advocate of Scotland issued a Summons to initiate the process of the 'Division of the Commonty of Holm Parish'.[35] In addition to Alexander Sutherland Graeme, ten other persons were also listed as having claims to the common lands, but all had relatively minor interests. On August 6, Irving, anticipating imminent division, gave Petrie precise instructions as to the proper manner of administering the division process from perambulation of the boundaries, searching out witnesses with knowledge of practices 'from time immemorial', erecting march stones, proper usage of Cess Books, etc.[36] Petrie once again exuded optimism when he wrote to the laird that division would be completed 'next year', though he was sufficiently prudent to mention that 'the Proprietors are not as One as to the disputed Marches'.

However, it was soon obvious that agents of the Crown were choosing to delay the division of the common lands of Holm. In the autumn of 1834 Irving informed Petrie that the Crown was seeking to sell these lands and was waiting for the best price.[37] Another complication arose on November 5, 1834, when John Ker, Agent of Lord Dundas, Earl of Orkney, filed a petition with the Sheriff Court, claiming that the commons of St. Andrews, St. Ola and Holm parishes were all part of one larger stretch of common land, in which the Earl had a significant interest. Petrie characterised this action as nothing more than an attempted land grab, having no merit whatever. He was also furious at the prospect that the delay would mean considerable expense for the estate. The factor expressed his outrage with the observation, 'Holm is not in the Earldom and Lord Dundas has not a single foot of land in the Parish'.[38]

Though Petrie and Irving achieved a significant victory in 1835 in having Lord Dundas's petition dismissed as 'incompetent' in the Sheriff Court, the dispute had a life of its own and was to linger on for several more years, taking on many different forms and, in effect, delaying the formal and legal division until 1844. This had a burdensome effect on the estate and prevented the implementation of some of the important improvement schemes in the interior of the parish. New land could not be brought into cultivation, fences, roads and drainage ditches could not be extended, new farms could not be created, etc.

When division of the commons finally did commence, with the issuing of the 'Report of the Commissioner in the Division of the Commonty of Holm' in 1844, it represented a near-total victory for the interests of the Graemeshall estate. The Report dismissed all claims put forward by the Crown and the Earldom and awarded the Graeme estate all rights to this huge parcel of land. A few plots, belonging to smallholders, most of whom were also tenants on the estate, were ceded by the Commission.[39] Thus, as a consequence of the division of the commons, Graeme was to own some nineteen-twentieths of the land within Holm parish.

The rights that were granted by this 30-page, hand-written document were fully in accordance with practices associated with notions of absolute private property that were growing ever more common on Orkney estates.[40] However, much of the language used and the arguments that the Commission employed had more in common with those of the customary rights and privileges of the recent past, and the Report does contain within its findings hints that it was partially receptive to claims based on custom and tradition, though these were clearly vestigial. For example, it recognised that the parish minister and the parish schoolmaster might continue to exercise their peat-cutting rights on the former common lands. But for ordinary tenants, cottars and crofters, once the common was divided, these rights belonged to the past.

These lands proved to be a great asset to the estate. Unfortunately, the records do not permit us to discover their precise allocation, except for one portion. In 1848, Mr. Thomas Traill, Esq., 7th of Holland, who owned immense portions of the island of Westray and all of neighbouring Papa Westray, purchased a vast tract of 1,200 acres of formerly virgin land in the Holm common to make up a large farm he called New Holland. This purchase could only have improved the fiscal situation of the Graemeshall estate, as well as providing it with a stimulating neighbour. By 1859, some 500 acres of this new estate were reclaimed and divided into 20-acre squared fields, enclosed by stone dykes. In 1871, the *Orcadian*, the local newspaper, singled out this property for special commendation. Considering it to be among the best managed in all the County, the newspaper proclaimed;

Mr. Traill is a gentleman of considerable agricultural experience—knows farming as a science, and is well-acquainted with it in practice and in detail, and has devoted much of his means and mental energy to the improvement of his native country.[41]

Much more of this former common land was also subsequently sold, for we shall observe that estate acreage was greatly diminished by the 1870s. As for the lands remaining within the estate, correspondence of the later 1840s suggests two trends, neither of which is surprising. On the one hand, existing practices continued for several years—unherded livestock roamed the still unfenced portion of the hills, peats were dug by all who felt the need for them, turf was scavenged and carried to farms, and building stones were sought by all who lived nearby. Some of the lands were therefore still available as a common resource. On the other hand, other parcels were attached to existing farms on the estate, fenced in and brought under the plough, generating additional rent for the estate. Cultivation moved steadily inwards and upwards from the coast.[42] Each year less of the common was available to the community in general and many residents of Holm felt this severely. Any surviving remnants of runrig farming could not have endured the loss of access to common grazing, nor could those communities that depended on it. All sources are in agreement that after 1857 tenants, cottars and labourers could no longer graze their stock on these common lands. Any other forms of customary usage would by then be considered trespass or usurpation and would have no basis in formal law. As is evident in the testimony provided in the Napier Commission Report in the 1880s, these losses stuck in the memories of the poorer tenants for generations. They vividly expressed their resentment.

5. Incessant Conflict Between Trustee and Factor

A modern business requires a clearly defined chain of command and a division of responsibilities. Neither of these arrangements was in place in Graemeshall during the years of improvement.

As we have seen, John Irving was the first to suggest improvement of the estate during the minority years of Alexander Sutherland Graeme. But once the process began, it was implemented and administered by the resident factor, David Petrie, Jr., whose approach to all things in life was so very different from that of Irving. Anyone perusing the hundreds of surviving letters between these two men from 1827 until 1850 can see that the correspondence was not a model of clear communication. They were locked into a pattern of disagreements and misunderstanding, and neither man was willing or able to adjust and adapt his ways in order to work effectively with the other. They met each other on only two occasions—in 1834 Irving visited Orkney, and in 1844 Petrie travelled to Edinburgh. No record survives of their face-to-face conversations. However, each was a permanent fixture in the life of the other.

For the first three years in their professional relationship, 1827–1830, both Irving and Petrie displayed a respectful tone in their correspondence. They appeared to work as partners in modernising a large estate, as is reflected in their moods of hopefulness and promise. However, late in 1830, as the kelp failed and the laird began his litany of requests for money, Irving's letters took on a sharper edge. He expressed impatience, for example, that he had received no money from Petrie for one year past, nor was it evident to Irving how rents were being applied toward improvement expenses. Irving concluded his letter with the demand, 'I would wish to have your accounts as factor up to the present time including of course the Rent of the Crop and Year 1829 examined and settled . . .'[43]

The following year, 1831, Irving repeatedly chided the factor for being unable to send Graeme a remittance, and he found Petrie's interminable delays in preparing and dispatching his accounts most irksome. In November, 1831 Irving had received the Accounts of Crops 1827 and 1828, but, unfortunately, Crop 1829 was still not yet ready. Irving became even more irate in expressing his dismay and frustration: 'You should have Crops 1828, 1829, 1830 in your hands. I am really disappointed you have sent no money. I can only account for you not doing this by your having taken the use of the money for yourself'.[44] The allegation that Petrie had made dishonest use of the rent money could not have been more direct, but it was also quite wide of the mark. Perhaps never in his career had Irving encountered such a peculiar mixture of practical competence and gross inefficiency in a single individual as he did in the case of David Petrie, Jr. The factor remained beyond the scope of Irving's understanding.

Petrie's response was that of a man deeply wounded. On December 6, in a lengthy letter, he provided Irving with a detailed accounting of the improvement expenses on the estate for the preceding three years. Unfortunately, this was the first time that Irving had seen any of these figures, even though he had directed that the improvements be made. Petrie revealed that the total improvement expenditures would probably total £1,600, a figure that proved to be reasonably accurate, but was also far more than Irving's prior estimate. The factor proceeded to reveal to Irving the enormous physical and psychological efforts he had made on behalf of the estate, constantly supervising the tenants, dealing with merchants and contractors, preparing for division of the commons, attempting to solve conflicts over Superior Duties, etc. Petrie concluded in a fit of exasperation:

> Had I been aware that Mr. Graeme's circumstances could not have admitted of this outlay, I never would have recommended any alteration from the old system . . . I should have been better off had it not taken place. I trust you will see that the observation . . . from your letter was uncalled for. It has given me much uneasiness and has hurt my feelings so much that I scarcely know what to say of it.

Since Petrie, like his father, prided himself on fulfilling the duties of a hard-working and loyal servant, the allegation hurt him deeply.

Irving's response was immediate. On December 16, he fully accepted the particulars of Petrie's account, but argued that the misunderstanding arose because of Petrie's extreme tardiness in completing his annual statements. He wrote that he was hopeful that the bulk of the expenses were in the past, and that Mr. Graeme's debts would soon abate. Unfortunately, a good working relationship between the two was never re-established.[45]

These conflicts persisted throughout 1832. The Edinburgh lawyer once again castigated the Orcadian factor on March 3 for incurring building expenses without first considering where the money would come from, particularly because some tenants were refusing outright to occupy the new steadings or to comply with the terms of their new leases. Nor did Irving feel that Petrie was sufficiently stern toward non-paying tenants. 'These should be got rid of as soon as may be', he admonished, 'but their Crop and Stock ought to be sold on behalf of the Proprietor . . .'[46] The year ended with Irving berating the factor for not having settled the nearly intractable problem of Superior Duties: 'I do not know of any good excuse you can have for your neglecting this matter'.

The staggering growth of Graeme's personal debts coloured most of the correspondence during 1833. It is evident that neither Petrie nor Irving could cope with the issue. Nonetheless, Irving consistently directed barbs of anger at Petrie for expenses incurred or for slowness of response. This period, however, was merely the calm before the storm.

By 1834, the estate experienced a deepening financial plight, a growing indebtedness and more difficulties with many tenants. On April 24, Irving informed Petrie that 'I am very much surprised to see from your accounts so very great an outlay on building expenses and that you have been borrowing money as factor. I am quite certain that by far too much has been laid out in buildings, on such very small farms . . . I am sure this will not be found profitable'. Petrie was guilty, according to Irving, of financial mismanagement.

By late May of that year, as the laird was under threat of imprisonment for non-payment, Petrie was tardy in furnishing a notarised rental list from the estate that had been demanded by Graeme's creditors and lawyers. On June 21, Irving unleashed a barrage of criticisms that concluded,' you see the evil you have done by neglecting to answer my letter and how much reason in these circumstances Mr. Graeme has to complain of your conduct'. Despite the dispatch of four more letters, Irving did not receive the rental list until July 24. Unfortunately, the list did not meet with Irving's satisfaction:

> I have received the Rental you have sent me, which on examining I find varies considerably from the Rentals sent with your Factory Accounts. . . . I have some intention of coming to Orkney with the Steam Vessel on 8 August next and if I do will be a day or two with you at Graemeshall about the 13th or 14th of the month.

There is no surviving account of their conversations in Graemeshall, but for much of the rest of the year their letters were on a more civil level. The rancour that had become so common was gone.

However, on March 25, 1835, Irving's frustration and anger boiled over once again. He complained:

> I am very much surprised indeed that you have not yet sent me any money or explained to me why money has not been sent . . . There must be something wrong in your management as Factor and it becomes my duty not to allow matters to continue longer on this present footing.

Unless Petrie could learn to be prompter with his payments, Irving concluded that he had no choice but to replace him as factor.[47] This is but one of thirty-two surviving letters that threatened Petrie with dismissal.

For the remainder of the year Irving repeated these threats, coupling them with detailed instructions concerning rent collection, how to report properly to the trustees, the method for rendering a correct account, etc. All of this was seemingly without effect. Should any of this have been necessary with a man of Petrie's family background and experience?

Yet on April 15, 1835, Irving's frustration increased still further when he wrote, 'On other estates where I take charge the Factor sends me the day after he collects the Rents a State of the Money received at each Collection and at the same time sends a Bank Receipt for the Amount to me. How widely different is your Mode of proceeding!' Several more letters followed, instructing Petrie in his duties, obligations and proper procedures.

Petrie was obviously incapable of altering his behaviour. Nonetheless, he was 'sincerely sorry to give cause to complain' and went to great lengths to promise, on April 29, to be prompt and clear in his disclosures and also to respond to each and every part of Irving's letters. Yet the litany continued as before. On September 7, 1835 Irving wrote to John Spence of the Commercial Bank of Kirkwall that

> Mr. Petrie is so very slow in everything that I have yet seen that I have had occasion to write him again and again without effect and have been obliged to inform that if this Bond of Caution [with respect to the laird's debts] is not sent me immediately I will have to appoint another Factor.

By October of 1835, Irving's criticism escalated: 'I really cannot submit to be trifled with in this manner any longer . . . you deceive yourself if you think I am going to put off doing this [replacing Petrie] any longer if you persist in paying no attention to what you have been required so often to do . . .'

This agonising exchange continued for the rest of the year but—despite Petrie's efforts to obey—circumstances remained much as before. Though stung by the criticism, Petrie's character was quite immutable in this area. By this point, Irving was doing no more than following an established routine.

Neither the years 1836 nor 1837 saw a change in the relationship between the two men. In the midst of destitution among the tenants and the economic plight of the estate, the disharmony and squabbling continued, lasting without a break to the end of the decade.[48] Petrie was repeatedly reprimanded and threatened with dismissal, yet he continued to remain employed as factor.

The 1840s witnessed continuing agricultural improvements on the estate, accompanied by a distinct upturn in the economy of Orkney. Though the surviving documentation thins out for this decade, on July 10, 1848, on the dawn of agricultural prosperity for Graemeshall and for Orkney, Petrie wrote to Irving:

> It would be a dreadful thing for me to be superseded by the appointment of another Factor after all the trouble I have had with the Matters of the Estate, and while all of the Energies of my Mind lie in furthering in everyway the Improvement of the Parish and Lands.[49]

As Petrie wrote this, it was not only apparent that the worst was over, but also that the estate was beginning to be held up as a model for others in Orkney to follow. The land was becoming more valuable and prospective tenants were eager to secure a lease on the property.

David Petrie remained as factor of Graemeshall and the properties in St. Ola parish for nearly eleven more years following John Irving's death in 1850. In 1861 the trustees of the estate replaced the 73-year-old factor with John Armit Bruce. Bruce served as factor until he was found drowned in Scapa Flow on May 26, 1883. Speculation centred upon his having fallen victim to an attack of asthma at the time.[50] He was subsequently replaced by A. J. Gold. Petrie continued to remain a local fixture, maintaining his tenancy on the farms of Graemeshall, Newtown and East Graves almost until his death in 1869. While his name appears on the surviving Rental of 1865, no mention is made of him in any estate rental after 1870.

Unfortunately for Petrie, his troubles with estate trustees did not end with Irving's death. The records testify to a continuing stream of complaints concerning his quixotic style of management and record keeping. Nonetheless, this negative image was tempered by the fact that he was also regarded both by the tenants and the other factors as a paragon and icon of agricultural improvement throughout Orkney.

Frustrated by their inability to obtain regular and reliable factory accounts from Petrie, the new trustees in Edinburgh were evidently on the verge of sacking him in November, 1851, when William Ranken, Procurator-Fiscal in Kirkwall, agent of the trustees and good friend of Petrie, energetically and eloquently interceded. He presented a very apt portrait of the factor:

> I have insisted that he shall lock himself up free from intrusions until the accounts are finished. I would certainly regret very much to see Mr. Petrie superseded. I have always esteemed him as a very worthy, honest man, who from his facility and kindness, and his inability to say *NO* has been preyed upon to a very large extent by kindred and would be friends. It is within my personal knowledge that he has done more towards the improvement of the Estate . . . than any other Proprietor in the County in the same space of time, and the Parish of Holm is now in consequence invariably pointed to as *THE* place where the greatest improvements have been achieved.

Ranken informed the trustees that virtually all of this improvement was achieved before the availability of government loans and other assistance.[51]

It is natural to wonder why David Petrie was retained as factor of the estate despite more than thirty years of dissatisfaction, complaints and threats of dismissal on the part of his superiors. Did he have a value that was unexpressed in writing? Possibly appointment of an outsider would have doomed the prospects for improvement, since such a person might never have been accepted by tenants who were threatened by the direction of the changes being made. Since tenant co-operation was so tentative, particularly in the early years of improvement, and since unrest of a more overt sort was always a possibility, it is entirely reasonable to suppose that during the early stages of improvement, David Petrie's role as factor was a key to the success of the entire project. On an estate in which the laird was a distant and abstract figure who commanded no personal loyalty, Petrie, a local man, was the only visible evidence of authority, stability and trust. After all, Petrie's father, mother, two brothers and his sisters were all buried in the Holm church graveyard, not to mention the fact that several other members of the Petrie family served as tenants on the estate.

Yet Petrie's slipshod methods of cost accounting had a ruinous effect on his personal fortunes. In a letter to Irving on July 2, 1849, the factor mentioned rather substantial arrears in his own rental to the estate and expressed his gratitude for the 'Patience and Forbearance' that was extended to him. Always the dutiful servant, he concluded, 'I feel I can never do too much for Mr. Graeme and you'.[52] The irony is that Petrie's fortunes fell at precisely the moment when those of the estate rose.

The aforementioned document entitled 'Memorandum respecting the Graemeshall Trust', dated March 1860, reveals the conflict between Petrie and the trustees during the 1850s. Clearly their level of frustration in dealing with him was as high as was Irving's. The trustees believed that Petrie prevented them from paying off the heritable debt by his sluggishness in remitting rents and the delays in rendering factory accounts. They were willing to give him the credit due for having been 'very successful in so far as regards the agricultural improvement of the property'. Nonetheless, they cite Irving's 'constant fight' with him for his accounts. Had the new trustees been able to follow their own inclinations, they would 'long ago have put in execution against Mr. Petrie the most stringent legal measures', but were blocked from such a course when 'Mr. Graeme interposed to prevent this,—he being of opinion that Mr. Petrie's local knowledge and agricultural skill were of great importance'. The Trustees were compelled to conclude that 'they do not see how the management of the Estate can be carried on with any degree of propriety and efficiency if Mr. Petrie is to be allowed to continue to act as Factor'.[53] It is remarkable that at the time this document was composed, the trustees had not received a formal rental from Petrie since 1852. All they had in their possession at that moment was Petrie's estimate that the 1859 Rental would be £1,369, or a substantial increase of £463 over the rental seven years before.

The trustees were similarly vexed to discover, years after the event, that Petrie 'without any authority whatever' had purchased for £150 the Mill of Scapa (site of the present distillery), which was at that time totally surrounded by the estate. This inability to control or predict Petrie's behaviour, or to gain any insight into the current financial affairs of the property, enabled the trustees to overcome the laird's objections and begin the process of removing the elderly factor from the position he had held for thirty-four years. Nevertheless, they allowed him to remain as tenant on the largest farm on the estate and to continue to reside for a time in the old mansion house.[54]

The final records of Petrie's life are indeed unfortunate. The estate papers contain a copy of a petition, with the signatures of Alexander Sutherland Graeme, Esq. and John Armit Bruce, Factor, dated March, 1868, which discussed the details of the impending bankruptcy of the 80-year-old David Petrie, Jr. Though Petrie's annual rental totalled £93, he was at that time hopelessly in arrears for the amount of £199. The petition acknowledged that 'the Respondent is in very embarrassed circumstances' and requested that an inventory be taken of 'said lands and farms and livestock, horses and sheep, corns and crops, to be held in security for payment'. In addition, Petrie assigned his 'whole property' in the event of his death, with 'deep gratitude', to Graeme, who acted as sole executor.[55] Thus Petrie was given a meagre measure of reward and indulgence for a lifetime of service to the estate. He was allowed to live out his days on the estate, maintaining a degree of dignity, but was unable to pass on to his cousins and nephews, who continued to farm on the estate, any earthly property. As a man imbued with the mentality of a loyal servant, Petrie appears to have been grateful for this solution. Most likely he felt that he had received his just rewards.

6. Greater than Anticipated Expenses in Implementing Improvement

The failure of anyone in authority on the Graemeshall estate to anticipate the expenditures connected with improvement of the property, from 1827 on, is nothing short of astonishing. As we shall see, John Irving never saw a proper estimate until after the estate had already contracted for a full round of obligations. The impression one gains from reading the surviving record is that the improvement of these lands was motivated by a near-religious (or ideological) faith in the improvement process itself, the assumption being that rewards would automatically appear, once the initial steps were undertaken. Unfortunately, this failure of anticipation would lead to years of bitterness, as the estate and its managers strove to climb out of the depths of indebtedness. During the late 1820s and 1830s there was never a time when the element of predictability was present. John Irving, the trustee, could at any time find himself the unexpected recipient of a major bill from Petrie in Orkney that required immediate attention, an urgent request for funds from the laird in England, or another demand from the Earldom or the Crown for a payment of those perpetually disputed Superior Duties.

The estate correspondence during the first few years of improvement, as could be expected, focused on the techniques and procedures required to modernise the estate, i.e. how to survey the land, construct the new inland roads, handle legal matters, dig ditches and drains, manage nervous tenants, etc. How to pay for this was never a prime topic, nor was there any interchange on the overall costs of the project. The absence of prior speculation on this matter is a clear failure of management on the part of all parties – Petrie, Irving and Graeme. In addition, the improvement model actually employed, i.e. construction of major projects at estate expense, was contrary to both Samuel Laing's prior advice and the subsequent practice of Colonel David Balfour.

It was only on November 29, 1829, after the estate had

committed itself to employ the surveyor and numerous Kirkwall merchants and contractors, that Petrie sent to Irving a proper estimate of expenses for the erection of new farm steadings (houses, barns, etc.) for the tenants. Though the expenditure on dwellings on the farm of Lingro in St. Ola parish alone amounted to £783, or a sum greater than the annual rental for all of Mr. Graeme's lands in Orkney (£715), the figures aroused no concern from John Irving at the time. Petrie did not yet have final figures for new farm steadings on the rest of the estate. However, this proved to be an early warning that was ignored by all concerned.[56] Apparently there was an underlying assumption that all of these costs would later be covered by higher rents (hopefully more than doubling within a decade).

The mood of confidence continued for most of 1831. It is true that there were many distracting elements that prevented anyone from closely examining expenses, i.e. the decline of the kelp industry, the division of the commons, Superior Duties, Mr. Graeme's perpetual pleas for money, not to mention the conflict between Petrie and Irving. However, on December 6, 1831, in a previously mentioned lengthy letter in which he was compelled once again to defend his behaviour, Petrie, for the very first time, outlined for Irving the amounts of money already committed or paid out. Petrie estimated that 'total improving expenses will probably be about £1,600'.[57] These figures, which proved to be fairly accurate, were acknowledged by Irving, who on December 16 of that year tersely noted that they were higher than he had ever imagined they would be. Perhaps he did not feel it necessary to sound a cry of alarm because crop prices had not yet begun to plummet.

By early 1832 Irving began to have forebodings of disaster. On February 14 of that year, Petrie informed Mr. Graeme that he had found it necessary to borrow money to pay the contracted workmen who were building the farm steadings. Early in March, Irving reacted with anger and surprise upon learning that Petrie had built the steadings without first considering where the money would come from. At that moment the prices for cattle were dropping, several tenants were resisting the newly-devised lease arrangements and the surveyor was threatening Petrie with legal action for non-payment of a four-year-old bill.[58]

During the following year, 1833, the estate was quite hard pressed to come up with the money for a huge (and disputed) assessment of £180 for Superior Duties. In addition, the larger farms on the estate were being encumbered as security for the laird's personal debts. A sense of anxiety pervaded Graeme's and Irving's letters to Petrie on all fiscal matters.[59]

By 1834, the economic problems had intensified in all respects. For example, the estate was still unable to pay the remainder of the bill owed to Grainger and Miller, Surveyors, for a total sum of £40, including accrued interest, for work that had been completed in 1828. The other chronic problems, ranging from the laird's debts, falling grain prices, tenant resistance, and delays in dividing the commons, were all still present. In April, 1834 Petrie sent to Irving a lengthy document entitled 'Expense of Survey and of Outlay on Farm Houses and Steadings and on the Improvement on the Estate of Graemeshall between 1828 and 1834'. A simplified breakdown follows for the three categories of costs:

1. All expenses relating to the survey paid until 1834: £160.
2. Expenses for farm steadings in St. Ola: £783.
3. Expenses for new steadings on 20 farms in Holm parish (farm by farm):

Gutterpool	£130
North House	81
Millfield	152
Rowland	149
Easterbister	60
Biggings	54
West Breckness	6
West Graves	6
East Graves	10
Quoylet	4
Air	4
Westwall	1
New Green	3

Vigga	3
East Breakin	11
Flaws	57
South House & Netherbow	14
Nether Breakquoy	18
Little House	29
Other Expenses	58
TOTAL EXPENDITURE:	£1,746
[corrected figure:	£1,803]

In examining these payments, one must note that the gross rental of all of the Sutherland Graeme lands in Orkney in the year 1834 amounted to no more than £877.[60] Though virtually all improvements were made on the supposition that the estate would base its economy on the export of live beef cattle to the markets near Aberdeen, no regular steamship service to the south yet existed. While Graemeshall was doling out these huge sums of money, the other lairds had only begun to speculate about how the steamship might benefit the Orkney economy. For example, in 1833, James Baikie, merchant and laird of Tankerness, distributed to all 'Gentlemen of Orkney and Caithness' a printed circular letter promoting the use of a fast, regular steamship service to ship live cattle to mainland markets. However, this was not available until after 1836, when the 378-ton paddle steamer, the *Sovereign*, was put into service.[61] Furthermore, Graemeshall improvement expenses were, for the most part, undertaken before government loans were available for this purpose by the Public Money Drainage Act in 1846. O'Dell provides the names of those lairds who were able to borrow a portion of the £20,000 allotted to Orkney (most significantly, £6,000 to David Balfour and £1,000 to Archer Fortescue).[62] The name of the laird of Graemeshall was not on this list. Nor could the estate take much advantage of the Orkney Roads Act of 1847. Orkney's economy entered into years of depression, starting in 1833, at precisely the moment when Graemeshall's expenditures reached the highest peaks already described.[63] Given this situation, the estate was fortunate indeed to remain a going concern during Orkney's most prosperous years of the century, 1848–1871. Thus, because of the disastrously premature start, the modernisation of Graemeshall estate was slow to bear fruit: the link between improvement and profit was tenuous indeed.

It is therefore not at all surprising that during the lean years of the late 1830s John Irving began to despair of the estate ever succeeding. In January, 1837, when many tenants suffered horrendous destitution, he noted: 'I do not think that farms should be let for less than £30 or £40. There would not be enough left for the Proprietor. Here [referring to the Lothians] we would consider £100 a small farm and be averse to building houses for farms which did not yield double that amount . . . There are evidently too many subdivisions of land on Graemeshall Estate'. He proceeded to urge that the numerous small farms of £8–10 rental be given up and combined with larger ones nearby. Yet few decisive moves in that direction were ever undertaken by either Irving or Petrie. By November, Irving evidently feared that all was about to be lost. He suggested to Petrie that Orkney's fate would not differ from that of the West Highlands, with 'its redundant population, no employment, loss of kelp and massive emigration'.[64] Only during the 1840s did Irving's pessimism show signs of lifting, as cattle sales grew, arrears of rent dropped, and tenants began to value their farms. It was also during this decade that Irving revealed the first glimmers of insight into how very different farming in Orkney was compared to the fertile Lowlands around Edinburgh.

7. Resistance of Tenants to Improvement

The words and thoughts of the poorer residents of the Graemeshall estate are seldom recorded in the surviving documents. Consequently our desire to lift the veil hiding the material circumstances of the hundreds of cottars, crofters and wage labourers who resided in Holm parish is probably doomed to frustration. All too often we do not even know their names. One can only hunger for direct primary materials, in the form of farm journals, diaries, etc., such as those recently utilised so successfully by Alun Howkins in his study of English agriculture.[65] Nor do we possess direct testimony from the tenants on the estate who held leases directly from the laird, though we do know their names, can link them with specific farms and can trace a few patterns in their behaviour. Rent payments, deliveries in kind for Superior Duties, farm tenure notations are all helpful. Petrie and Irving always made it a point to monitor and discuss how the tenants reacted to the improvements and their new lease arrangements, for they knew that success was dependent upon the tenants sharing their vision. They promptly discussed any overt sign of tenant discontent, although they rarely explained it to a historian's satisfaction. In the absence of any effective local compulsory apparatus, those in authority knew that ultimately improvements depended upon a large degree of agreement and co-operation. There was evidently great reluctance to employ the ultimate sanction, eviction of tenants. Such harsh measures were much less frequent throughout Orkney than on the Scottish mainland.

The estate papers covering the factorship of David Petrie, Senior, from 1782 until 1827, contain no hints of overt conflict between landlord and tenant. Records are exceptionally complete for an Orkney estate during this period, with a seemingly endless stream of letters exchanged between Petrie and the Admiral until 1818, and, thereafter, with John Irving until 1827. The Admiral was not a very exacting landlord, and the tenants seemed to be compliant and respectful toward a man who was a distant but admired figure. They also appear to have been left to their own devices. The Admiral's interest in the affairs of the estate did not extend much beyond the subject of kelp, though he did always respond to letters about hardship in the lives of the tenants. If a favour was in his power to grant, he did so willingly. No change in this relationship is apparent during the minority of Alexander Sutherland Graeme, from 1818 to 1827.

For the tenants of Graemeshall, agricultural improvement was a leap in the dark. They were asked to embrace a world that had not yet been born. To examine the problem from another perspective, the tenants were called upon to abandon nearly all of their customary agricultural practices, so that a new system, hitherto absent from Orkney, could be imported from faraway Edinburgh. Though they were told that the 'New Style' farming represented opportunity, they were also well aware that it represented a certain loss of independence, i.e. that they would now be dependent on their access to capital (new equipment, seed, lime, more horses, purchase of fertiliser, etc.) and markets in ways that were quite new to them. Coupled with the steady loss of access to the common lands and the decline of their proto-industries, the tenants on the estate viewed their future as one of increasing dependence on the landlord and his servants. Not only would the new rents be far higher than previously, but they would be collected with an unaccustomed timeliness and efficiency. Finally, it was apparent that tenure on the estate would depend on productivity and compliance. The tenants evidently approached the task with trepidation and could only greet the promises of these near-miraculous improvements in their future with a healthy dose of scepticism.

Assuredly, the soil of Orkney was uniquely rich and fertile for this northern region, the landscape gentle and the climate mild. But tenants also knew how changeable their climate could be—cold, wet summers could prevent the grain from ever ripening, as could a summer of drought. There was the ever-present possibility of a late spring that could be calamitously followed by an early autumn. A fickle climate only increased the risks and uncertainties associated with agricultural improvement. We must also take note of the distance from markets, a labour force inexperienced in the new ways, and the attitudes of a people who found more profit in their proto-industrial by-employments than they did in their farming.

Although the tenants were always lured with positive inducements and promises of reward, they also faced another stark reality—the economic slump of the 1830s. During that period entire families emigrated from Orkney, and young men regularly sought out careers with the Hudson's Bay Company in Canada, the whaling fleet in the Davis Straits, the fishing industry or the Royal Navy. Those remaining at home all too often found themselves in conflict with their landlords. As the promises of prosperity on Graemeshall estate began to look ephemeral, such conflict became inevitable, though it was somewhat circumscribed because of the insularity and traditions of the community. Violent confrontation was simply not a part of the Orcadian character. Orkney was too remote to follow such English altercations as the Swing riots, nor do the 'underground' resistance traditions described by Howard Newby seem to be present.[66] Confrontation tended, instead, to be inspired by religious nonconformity. For example, early nineteenth-century dissidents joined the Secession Church rather than remain loyal to the 'Auld Kirk', which accepted the patronage of the lairds. Only when signs of prosperity returned, early in the 1840s, did large numbers of tenants begin to accept fully their new lease arrangements and obligations. New people from outside Orkney also sought to obtain leases on the estate. Those who held improving leases then worked enormously hard to increase the value of their property and to implement the new techniques that were part of the emerging agricultural system.[67]

Several documents to be found in the Sutherland Graeme papers describe the intentions of Irving and Petrie, the obligations of the tenants and the difficulties that occurred in implementing the improvements. For example, on November 1, 1830 a printed handbill, signed 'Alexander Sutherland Graeme, Esquire of Graemeshall', offered cash premiums to those tenants who made four basic improvements in their lands:

1. To those who brought 'into proper cultivation the most Break, or Waste Land' during the course of a single year.
2. To those who cultivated 'the greatest quantity of Turnips properly hoed and manured'.

3. To the tenant who 'most improved his Farm by covered or open drains'.
4. To the tenant who 'has most improved his Farm by liming during the year'.[68]

Even more explicit are three printed improving leases, at the time unusual in the Orkney Islands, that have survived from among the seventy-three issued on the estate from 1831 until 1836. Two of the leases, issued on August 16, 1831, were held by Edward Copland for the farm of Quoymay, made up chiefly of brecklands of 35 acres, and by John Shearer for the farm of Donnersbrae, 19 acres arable plus 12 acres of breckland. The third lease, issued on July 31, 1836, was held jointly by John Wilson and Robert Sclater, both originally from the nearby isle of Sanday, for the more substantial farm of Millfield, which consisted of 73 acres. As noted, the estate had erected a new steading on this farm at a cost of more than £152.[69] It is indeed striking how exceedingly specific these leases are in defining the rights, obligations and privileges of each tenant, and how the lease directed farming practices during its entire duration. Also noteworthy is the fact that the lease employed language and terminology that made it read like a hybrid between a feudal document and a modern business contract, i.e. 'to which the Lands hereby let may be thirled', meaning that the tenant was bound to use the laird's mill.

The stipulations of these leases left little to chance, or to the caprice of the farmers who held them. One notices all the rights reserved for the proprietor, i.e., the right to pasture on the hill ground, 'whole Quarries, Mines and Minerals', all rights to kelp and fishing, etc. The farmer could only make use of the kelp for manure if it was first driven by wind and tide upon the shore. The farmer was entitled solely to the produce of the soil, but was obliged to maintain all houses, drains, roads and fences in good condition.

The main aim of these leases was the improvement of the farms. They stated explicitly that '. . . the Tenant hereby binds and obliges himself . . . to crop and manage the

Arable Lands and Meadow Ground hereby let, according to the Rules of good Husbandry'. The document then proceeded to define precisely how the land was to be tilled, crops rotated and grown, which break lands were to be brought under the plough, etc. Strong emphasis was always placed on the waste lands, on root crops, such as potatoes and turnips, and on the cultivation of green grasses. 'During the last two years, the Tenant is to have as much Land in Green Crop . . . and *not* to have more of the Farm under Corn or White Crop . . . and is *not* during these last two Years to break up any Pasture or Lea Ground, without laying down an equal quantity of the arable Land to Grass.'[70] Simply translated, tenants were required to work toward the transition from cereal crops (oats and bere) to rearing livestock on local pasture land, for live export to the mainland of Scotland.

The tenants were closely bound to the terms of their leases, which had three phases: 1. For a period of five years, no increase in rent and the tenant was free to quit *after* this period, following a written request, with one year's notice, with the permission of the proprietor. 2. The next five-year period was to begin in 1835 and called for a rent increase, hopefully £180 for the entire estate, with the tenants having the same right to quit at the end of this period. 3. The third period was to begin in 1840 and called for the tenantry to pay a total rent £308 above that which they paid at the start of the process.[71] There can be little dispute that, in theory, the tenant bore the more perilous share of the bargain. However, in practice, the laird was also taking a considerable risk, and the factor's task was thankless.

Serious difficulties arose even before the leases went into effect. For example, in April, 1829 Petrie felt it necessary to inform the laird that the Reverend Andrew Smith, the longtime parish minister of Holm, 'has done everything in his Power to oppose the Improvement of your Estate both when the Surveyor was here and since . . .', while in November of the same year Petrie wrote to Irving that several tenants and Mr. Smith were 'clearly threatened by and hostile to the Survey and Divisions'.[72] Another ominous sign appeared on June 25, 1830, even before copies of the printed leases arrived from Edinburgh, when the estate tenants dispatched a petition to Irving, objecting to the projected amounts of the rent and the terms of payment. Furthermore, they requested an 'indulgence' of from six to nine months for payment of arrears and that the laird grant the tenant the right to give up his farm automatically after five years. They regarded the obligation of tenants to provide peats and lodging to kelp workers on the shores as unduly burdensome, particularly since such kelp was the exclusive property of the laird. Finally, the tenants demanded that the number of days on which they were subject to labour services, for the purpose of building roads, bridges, digging ditches, etc. be limited. In response to this petition, Irving did grant the tenants an indulgence on the arrears.[73] Beyond that he would not go. It is evident from this exchange that the tenants were not optimistic about their prospects under the new agricultural regime. Not only were they deeply suspicious about the entire enterprise, they most likely also held very different notions of property rights and obligations.

The first full calendar year in which the improving leases were in effect, 1831, saw no outbreaks of protest, or large-scale lack of co-operation with the administrators. Numerous complaints about individual tenants found their way into the estate correspondence. Irving was particularly piqued by tenants who continued to allow their livestock to wander freely and trespass onto others' fields. The old ways were incompatible with the new in Graemeshall. He suggested to Petrie that he sternly warn these offending tenants and, if necessary, he should 'poind' (seize) their cattle. He also urged that tenants continue to be encouraged to plant the required turnips and grass seeds.[74] All of this strongly implies that tenant efforts fell far short of what those in authority expected of them.

During 1832, tenant protest moved from words to deeds. On March 3 Irving was most distressed to have to deal with six tenants who resolutely declined to occupy their farms, even though new steadings had been erected at estate expense. He chided Petrie for not 'binding' these tenants in ways that would have prevented such an occurrence. Irving, regarding the situation as out of control, offered the following observation and solution:

> It is setting an exceedingly bad example to allow tenants who are at all able to pay . . . to throw up their farms when they please unless they receive an abatement of rent and on that account ought never to be done. It is otherwise where tenants cannot pay. These ought to be got rid of as soon as may be but their stock and crop ought to be sold on behalf of the Proprietor.[75]

By this date a pattern emerged that was to hold firm for many years. Irving was to minimise consistently the plight of all tenants and residents on the estate, insist on their ability to fulfil all obligations, and looked upon any contract as fixed and immutable. He was suspicious of the motives of all tenants who made their fears and wishes known to him. Petrie, on the other hand, often assumed the role of explaining to Irving the local circumstances and the actual situation of the tenants, though he never acted as their advocate in opposition to the trustee. Always deferential to authority, Petrie was never the overt protagonist of either class or regional interests.

As the economy turned downward the following year, the tenants' predicament only worsened—their produce prices dropped and they found it far harder to pry money from the hill cottagers. Fulfilment of the terms of their lease became an ever more remote possibility. The autumn of 1833 was a particularly bad time for all. On October 24 Petrie remarked that the tenant James Maxwell of Ferry Inn was deeply in arrears, unable to pay his rents and was without funds. When the factor proposed to Irving the seizure of his entire crop and farm animals, his observation inadvertently provided a measure of how circumstances had changed: 'This will be the first sequestration for debt that has ever taken place on the Estate of Graemeshall, but there is no avoiding it at the present case'.[76]

Other problems kept appearing. The farm of Rowland

was given up by the tenant, James Aim, and was then advertised to let, but no offers appeared. Petrie advised Irving to permit Aim to stay as a tenant-at-will, since otherwise the farm would remain empty. In addition, William Tait was unhappy with his rent at Millfield and offered £16 to continue farming his 41 acres. Since the highest alternative offer was only £14, Tait also remained at will.

Other tenants protested in a manner that bordered on hostility to the entire new arrangement. Petrie wrote to Irving that several of the smaller tenants, led by Peter Langskaill of Hilltop and James Copland (whose lease we examined), surreptitiously cut peats at night, in clear defiance of the rules, and hid them in the home of the Secession Church minister, Mr. Buchanan (this would have been the Reverend Peter Buchan). The peats seem to have been intended for the minister's personal use. Copland was singled out for further commentary. Not only did he openly proclaim that he paid the lowest rent on the entire estate (he was actually incorrect), but he steadfastly refused to improve the breaklands as required in the lease. Petrie, plainly irked, protested to Irving, '. . . this is the Manner in which he is ignorantly shewing his independence for a brief period, but if he does not submit to any terms . . . a prohibition to send Cattle to the Hill [common lands] will speedily bring him to terms or ruin him'.[77] The level of threat perceived is most interesting. Despite the absence of other records, one is compelled to speculate that the discontent on the estate was very high, given the prominence given to a few overt cases in the official correspondence. As poorer tenants, these individuals were least likely to benefit from these changes. It is also likely that they saw the Reverend Buchan as their advocate.

The year 1833 came to an end with Petrie presiding over a meeting of Mr. Graeme's tenants. Most were perturbed over how they would meet their rents, scheduled to rise in 1835. Petrie informed the tenants that the leases would in no way be altered. He did suggest, however, that the tenants were unable to pay because they had failed to conform to the terms of their leases, i.e., not enough green crops planted, very few specialised breeds of cattle (beef and diary), insufficient usage of the hills, lack of winter herding, etc. He informed the tenants that their projected rents were based on their raising more cattle, potatoes and turnips than they were presently doing, and he repeated that the traditional Orkney crops such as oats and bere could never produce the amount of cash necessary to pay rent on an improving lease. Yet in a weak market, with declining prices, many tenants were unable or unwilling to commit their wellbeing and that of their families to what they considered to be a risky venture. However, Petrie concluded his letter to Irving by mentioning that several of the more productive tenants expressed the wish that the estate would rigorously and consistently enforce the terms of the leases for *all* tenants. It appears therefore that although a few tenants could successfully make the transition from one system to another, the bulk of the tenantry attempted to straddle both forms of agriculture simultaneously. Agricultural modernisation was producing a new form of differentiation among the estate's residents.

Early in 1834 Irving responded to these developments in a mood of frustration:

> I am of the opinion the conditions of their leases should be *enforced*. Their cattle ought to be poinded if they will not herd them in winter and they should be charged on their tacks [leases] to implement the terms. The Sheriff ought to be brought in if necessary. No tenant who has willfully neglected to have a portion of his land in green crops should get any favours.[78]

Irving's draconian response does not demonstrate an intimate understanding of the type of society with which he was dealing, nor does he display an appreciation of the source of the problem. The fact that the price of bere, the local barley, was only one half the retail rate for 1829/30 never seemed to have entered into his calculations. Though stern pronouncements readily flowed from Irving's pen, he acted upon them only rarely.

The estate rental for 1834 included a new category of farms not found on any previous rental, 'Lands not under Lease'. It is important to note that of the eleven farms so listed, five of them had had new steadings erected on them, at considerable expense, during the years 1828–1831.[79] Although the total cost of these five steadings amounted to about £636, the combined annual rental from all eleven of these farms came to a mere £135. These figures provide startling evidence of the failure of the improvement process on the estate to date, since not even improvement costs could be recouped in a reasonable period of time, let alone permit the estate to reap a clear profit. Furthermore, it is increasingly apparent that a combination of economic crisis and tenant resistance prevented the full implementation of the plans for improvement. It is likely that these plans were *never* fully achieved, which would account for the continued presence of very small, uneconomic tenancies on the estate throughout our period.

As the farm crisis deepened in 1835, several of the tenants-at-will were compelled to abandon all of their property and depart from their farms—James Aim left the farm of Rowland, William Tait could no longer continue at Millfield, nor could John Spence remain in Biggins or James Wylie keep the farm of Muckle Hunclet. Even tenants with leases reached the very limit of their ability to cope in that year. James Maxwell of Ferry Inn gave up his farm, while Ann Garrioch, who lived on the very small property of Valdigen with her son, a minor, declined to pay her rent. Another female tenant residing on a tiny farm, Barbara Taylor of West Moss, resided with her poor sister and daughter. Petrie noted: 'Her daughter continues insane and is more or less violent occasionally'. Petrie avoided any recommendation as to her fate, though her name does not appear anywhere on the 1840 estate rental.[80]

Unfortunately, the surviving record for 1836 is too sparse for specific commentary, although there is no evidence that economic circumstances had somewhat improved. In August, 1837 Petrie prepared a list of eleven tenants whom he felt would be unable to pay their rents upon completing the October harvest. Irving chose three from that list for prompt removal. Irving once more vented his frustration that the estate was too subdivided with small farms and noted that, in his opinion, no annual rental ought to be under £40–50.[81] Since the largest rental at that time was only slightly more than £25, such a policy, if implemented, would have resulted in the removal of each and every tenant on the estate. Had that policy been in effect in the year 1840, only two of the sixty-four tenants would have been permitted to remain. Irving's suggestion thus once again raises the question of how well he understood the realities of farming in an island community at the northern end of Britain, or how aware he was of the hardships associated with this serious economic downturn. His consciousness seems to have come to a halt on the bottom line of a bookkeeper's ledger.

Much of the estate correspondence for the latter 1830s and the 1840s no longer survives, though other sources do inform us of a slow upturn in the Orkney economy by 1840 and throughout the decade. Estate records are silent concerning the effects of the potato crop failure of the late 1840s that afflicted large parts of Scotland. But by 1849 there is no more discussion of tenant removal on Graemeshall Estate. Farmers from outside the islands, in possession of capital and skills, sought to obtain leases on the estate, as did a few of the smaller neighbouring proprietors. Those tenants who were already there considered their leases to be quite valuable and, according to Petrie on July 2, 1849, they kept their lands in a 'high state of cultivation and are still progressing'. When Petrie informed seven of the tenants that they were to be offered brand new leases, beginning in 1850, the news 'awakened great joy in their various habitations'. The factor was also delighted to add that the tenants were then bringing large tracts of the former common lands under cultivation. One of the tenants receiving a new lease was William Tait of Nether

Breakquoy, the same man who had been removed from the farm of Millfield in 1835.[82] It would thus appear that at the end of Irving's life some of the beneficial changes he had wished to see on the estate twenty-two years earlier had finally come to pass.

The tenant who caused the greatest concern and who inspired the most discussion among Irving, Petrie and the laird was Thomas Mackenzie of Groundwater, who held a lease on the farm of Lingro, a very large stretch of land, over 242 acres, located in St. Ola parish about five miles north-west of Graemeshall. This fertile property was purchased by the Graeme family during the eighteenth century, primarily for the value of its long kelp-rich shoreline. Lingro stretched for a mile or so along the shores of Scapa Bay. On the surface, Mackenzie would seem to have been an ideal improving tenant. He evidently was a man of considerable energy, skill and imagination. Petrie acknowledged in December, 1833 that his prodigious efforts resulted in the cultivation of 50 acres of breakland, the adding of great quantities of lime annually to the soil and the cultivation of from 30–40 acres of turnips and potatoes. Mackenzie also cut, at his own expense, a road to the coast in order to cart up large quantities of seaweed for use as fertiliser. Petrie remarked with pleasure: 'I defie anyone to say there is a better managed farm in all the County'.[83] Yet on November 8, 1833 Mackenzie expressed his intention of giving up his lease (in 1835) unless his rent of £120 per annum were reduced to £84. Mackenzie mentioned that he had been compelled to lower the rents of his own tenants who were unable to pay at the higher rates. In addition, he had fallen £106 in arrears to the estate. He was thus unable to buck the tide of falling commodity prices.

Petrie stressed that Mackenzie was too valuable a tenant to lose and urged Irving to accept a reduced rental of £100–110 as fair and realistic. Irving, true to form, wanted to hold Mackenzie to the full 15-year lease and suggested that he be 'compelled' to remain and to fulfill *all* of its terms. Petrie, in March of 1834, had to remind

Irving of the tenant's right to quit after five years. Furthermore, he informed the trustee of all of the permanent improvements that Mackenzie had built on a rather neglected farm, i.e. a stable, garden wall and several other buildings, that all added to the estate's total value. He urged Irving to bear in mind that 'Large farms are not easily let at present on a short notice in Orkney owing to a great fall in the price of grain, and they will not let for nearly as much as they did in 1829 and 1830'. Included in this heavy dose of realism was Petrie's recommendation for a speedy decision, due to the need to plant the crop on time. However, both Irving and Graeme repeatedly postponed making a decision on the fate of the largest tenant on the property.

Finally, in April, 1835, Petrie wrote to Irving that Mackenzie had taken a new farm on the island of Stronsay, where land was fertile and rents were much cheaper. In addition, the tenant was planning to borrow £1,000 in Edinburgh and would pay off his arrears to the estate. The *New Statistical Account*, compiled in 1842, indicated that 'Mr. Mackenzie of Groundwater' was one of the principal landowners on Stronsay.[84] When Petrie proceeded to advertise for a new tenant for Lingro, he received no offer higher than £100 per annum. The estate rental for 1840 listed John Johnston as tenant for Lingro, paying an annual rental of £105, still considerably below that paid by Mackenzie in 1833.[85] If a man of Mackenzie's talents was unable to farm successfully on Graeme's property during the 1830s, it is apparent that the demands placed upon the tenants were wholly unrealistic for the moment. It also suggests that Petrie's assessment of the situation was much more realistic than Irving's. The latter's inflexibility and inability to make a decision led to the loss of the most valuable and capable tenant the estate was likely to attract. It further suggests that rents had been set far too high, probably reflecting the necessity of having the tenants pay for the enormous improvement expenses incurred during the years from 1828 until 1834.

One searches in vain for first-hand testimony indicating

how improvements directly affected the lives of Graeme's tenants, cottars, labourers, or their families. Nonetheless, two pieces of descriptive literature do offer some insight into living conditions in Holm parish during the early 1840s. In response to the frightful destitution of 1837, the Scottish Poor Law Inquiry Commission issued its report in 1843. The information is primarily an assembly of impressions—of widely varying accuracy and quality—of the state of the poor within the various parishes of Orkney. Some testimony barely rises above hearsay, but, at the same time, the report also contains observations rich in insight and compassion. Among those asked to give evidence were parish ministers, heritors, factors, doctors and a sheriff-substitute. Unfortunately, the Commissioners appear to have made no effort to interrogate those who were themselves the subjects of the inquiry: the poor of the county. The general impression one gains from reading the report is that Orkney was quite fortunate in comparison with Scotland as a whole, while Holm was a somewhat favoured parish within Orkney. The Reverend Peter Buchan of the Congregation of the United Associate Synod, reporting on the parish of Holm, noted that only 19 people required relief in 1835, 1836, and 1837. The parish population in the 1841 census was 866. In general, most other parishes reported a higher level of destitution. Nonetheless, Buchan offered the biting observation that 'It is my decided opinion that the provision made for paupers in all parishes throughout Orkney . . . is altogether inadequate for their support. It forms, indeed, in the parish with which I am connected, but an insignificant pittance'.[86] Buchan depicted a parish in which the few truly poor were quite dependent upon family and neighbours for sustenance, but he also felt that the minimum necessary for survival was generally provided. Only about three or four persons in the entire parish 'go about as beggars'. However, Buchan did recommend 'a small assessment levied for the benefit of the aged and infirm poor'. Though he made no attempt to relate poverty to the rapid modernisation efforts in the parish,

Buchan offered some interesting observations about living conditions in Orkney:

> The working population . . . are differently situated in Orkney from what they are in most of the other counties in Scotland. They have almost all small patches of land. They raise potatoes sufficient for the supply of their families, and most of them keep a cow and a pig, and a few of them have sheep. They have the peculiar advantage of having at all times access to the sea, and no man, if diligent, need be without a sufficient supply of fish for his family.

Finally, Buchan presented his assessment of the character of the Orcadians among whom he lived and worked. On the whole, he considered Orcadians to be somewhat indolent, noting: 'Activity, indeed, is not the peculiar characteristic of the inhabitants of Orkney'. However, and more positively, he remarked that Orcadians were a sober people, and observed: 'There is not an individual in the whole parish whom I would accuse of being a drunkard'. He was pleased to conclude his report by informing the Commission that they should regard the Orcadian people as, above all, a decidedly respectable lot.[87]

Though he was less concerned with the state of the poor in the parish, the Reverend Andrew Smith, in his contribution to the *New Statistical Account* in 1842, does provide some insight into daily life in Holm. He describes a community of small farmers experiencing a significant process of agricultural change and modernisation. Smith related these changes to a

> continual emigration of the young men . . . there being no employment on the farm for them. Most of the youth have no other means of living but engaging as hands on board of coasting vessels and revenue-cutters, or vessels trading to the Baltic and foreign countries, and few of them ever return.[88]

The resulting shortage of men in the population was typical of Orkney at this time. Smith also noted that the parish poor rolls carried the names of only 15 persons.

Notes

1 *New Statistical Account*, p. 67.
2 *Ibid.*, p. 146.
3 *Ibid.*, p. 185.
4 *Ibid.*, p. 102.
5 *Ibid.*, p. 218.
6 Thomson, *History of Orkney*, pp. 226–28.
7 O'Dell, p. 216.
8 *Ibid.*, pp. 223–224; Robert O. Pringle, 'On the Agriculture of the Islands of Orkney', *Transactions of the Highlands and Agriculture Society of Scotland*, 1874, pp. 17–23.
9 William P. L. Thomson, *Kelp-Making in Orkney* (Kirkwall, 1983).
10 OCA, D5/39/5.
11 Ibid., D5/12/6, D5/10/3; P. N. Sutherland Graeme, *The Orkney Herald*, September 23, 1952.
12 OCA, D5/10/5.
13 Thomson, *History of Orkney*.
14 OCA, D5/12/6.
15 Ibid., D5/4/2, D5/46/9.
16 Ibid., D5/4/4.
17 Ibid.
18 Ibid., D5/4/6.
19 Ibid., D5/10/2.
20 Ibid., D5/10/3.
21 Ibid., D5/10/4.
22 Ibid., D5/10/5.
23 Ibid., D5/10/4, D5/10/5.
24 Ibid., D5/10/6.
25 Ibid., D5/10/7.
26 Ibid., D5/4/1.
27 Ibid., D5/4/7. Donaldson's Hospital, founded by James Donaldson of Broughtonhall (1751–1830), Edinburgh printer, was designed to be a hospital for poor children, including those who were deaf. The Hospital (and the Donaldson Trust) still exist in Edinburgh, but it is now known as Donaldson's College for the Deaf. John Irving served as one of the original Donaldson trustees. It is most likely that John Donaldson was either the brother or the son of James Donaldson. I am grateful to William P. L. Thomson and R. P. Fereday for suggesting I examine this connection. Letters of June 7 and June 29, 1994, Lawrence D.

Marshall, Clerk and Treasurer, The Donaldson Trust, Donaldson's College, Edinburgh. Also E. F. Catford, *Edinburgh: The Story of a City* (Edinburgh, 1975), p. 59.

28 D5/4/6.

29 William P. L. Thomson, 'Common Land in Orkney', *Orkney Heritage.* Vol. 1, 1981, pp. 73–91.

30 *Ibid.*, pp. 82–83.

31 OCA, D5/33/13; Ronald Miller (ed.), *The Third Statistical Account of Scotland: The County of Orkney* (Edinburgh, 1985), p. 56.

32 OCA, D5/10/2.

33 Ibid., D5/10/4.

34 Ibid., D5/10/4.

35 Ibid., D5/3/12.

36 Ibid., D5/10/5.

37 Ibid., D5/4/1.

38 Ibid.

39 Ibid., D5/3/12.

40 E. P. Thompson, examining the division of common lands within a larger context, depicts 'a wholesale transformation of agrarian practices, in which rights are assigned away from users and in which ancient feudal title is compensated in its translation into capitalist property right'. Thus, 'we see exposed with unusual clarity the law's complicity with the ideology of political economy, its indifference to the claims of the poor, and its growing impatience with coincident use-rights over the same soil'. Thompson concludes with the observation that 'Security of property is complete only when commons come to an end'. E. P. Thompson, *Customs in Common: Studies in Traditional Popular Culture* (New York, 1993), pp. 137, 141 and 165.

41 *Orcadian*, February 26, 1871. It was not possible for the estate to sell parcels of land before 1848 since it was entailed. However, in that year Parliament passed Rutherford's Act which permitted heirs to disentail their estates and dispose of them at will. Much property in the hands of 'the effete gentry' was purchased by the newly rich: Michael Fry, *Patronage and Principle . . .*, p. 60.

42 OCA, D5/4/6; Alexander Fenton, *The Northern Isles: Orkney and Shetland* (Edinburgh, 1978), p. 95; Robert O. Pringle, 'On the Agriculture of the Islands of Orkney', *Transactions of the Highlands and Agriculture Society of Scotland* (Edinburgh, 1874), p. 55.

43 OCA, D5/10/4.

44 Ibid., D5/10/5. It is probably incorrect that Irving was accusing Petrie of theft. Petrie might have used the delay to pay off his own short-term debts, or perhaps loaned the money to relatives to tide them over a period of cash shortage.

45 Ibid.

46 Ibid., D5/10/6.

47 Ibid., D5/4/2.

48 Ibid., D5/4/3, D5/4/4.

49 Ibid., D5/4/6.

50 *Orcadian*, May 26, 1883. The article mentions that the 48-year-old Bruce also served as Sheriff-Clerk and was clerk to several local public trusts. In addition, the newspaper depicted him as a local antiquarian of some note. The Sheriff found suicide to be the cause of death, since Bruce died at a dreadful moment in the fortunes of the estate. It was already known that the Napier Commission would be taking testimony in Orkney. D5/30/4.

51 OCA, D5/4/7.

52 Ibid., D5/4/6.

53 Ibid., D5/4/7.

54 Ibid.

55 Petrie's name also appeared regularly in the Sherriff Court in Orkney. In February, 1868 the laird and factor sued him for failure to pay rent. Later his property was sequestered to pay the debt. In October, a Summons of Removing against him was raised. At that time he was described as being a tenant at will on the farms and lands of Graemeshall, East Graves and Newton, though he seems to have been living at Mayfield, St. Ola. OCA, SC11/5/1869/38, SC11/5/1869/24, SC11/5/1869/37. I thank Alison Fraser, Archivist, for this reference.

56 OCA, D5/10/3.

57 Ibid., D5/10/5.

58 Ibid., D5/10/6.

59 Ibid., D5/10/7.

60 Ibid., D5/12/6, D5/12/7.

61 Ibid., D5/3/17; Thomson, *History of Orkney*, p. 226.

62 O'Dell, pp. 199–200.

63 Thomson, p. 228.

64 OCA, D5/4/4, D5/4/5

65 Alun Howkins, *Reshaping Rural England: A Social History, 1850–1925* (London, 1991).

66 Howard Newby, *Country Life: A Social History of Rural England* (London, 1987).

67 E. P. Thompson has reflected on the absence of overt protest to dramatic changes in rural property relations and also observed that mention of them rarely made their way into the press. He proceeded to observe that 'They will be found . . . more often in the exchange of letters between estate stewards and their absent masters, treated as domestic concerns (like poaching) . . .' Most resistance, he observed, was 'more often sullen than vibrant' and 'One can turn up other affairs like this in collections of estate papers'. E. P. Thompson, *Customs in Common* pp. 115–117.

68 OCA, D5/3/13.

69 Ibid., D5/3/7, D5/4/3.

70 Ibid.

71 Ibid., D5/10/5.

72 Ibid., D5/10/3. Rev. Smith provided no hint of the basis of his opposition to these improvements. He certainly softened his enmity rather quickly and remained minister in the parish until 1855.

73 Ibid., D5/10/4.

74 Ibid., D5/10/5.

75 Ibid., D5/10/6.

76 Ibid., D5/10/7.

77 Ibid., Callum G. Brown has observed that the growth of the Secession Church in Scotland marched in tandem with the spread of agricultural improvement and frequently served as a vehicle for tenant protest. See Callum G. Brown, 'Religion and Social Change', in T. E. Devine and Rosalind Mitchison (eds.), *People and Society in Scotland, Vol. 1, 1760–1830* (Edinburgh, 1988), pp. 150–151.

78 OCA, D5/4/1.

79 Ibid., D5/46/9, D5/12/7.

80 Ibid., D5/4/2, D5/46/9.

81 Ibid., D5/4/2, D5/4/4.

82 Ibid., D5/4/6.

83 Ibid., D5/10/7.

84 *NSA*, Rev. John Simpson, 'Stronsay and Eday', p. 152.

85 OCA, D5/46/9.

86 *Poor Law Inquiry Commission for Scotland, Orkney* (1843), p. 242.

87 *Ibid.*

88 *NSA*, p. 220.

CHAPTER FIVE

Assessment of Estate Rentals

The surviving estate rentals provide a general indication of the economic fortunes of Graemeshall and how they fluctuated over the years. However, the idiosyncratic book-keeping methods employed preclude any application of refined statistical techniques. The early accounts are some-what less useful for our purposes than those completed later. For example, the Account Book of 1805, compiled by David Petrie, Sr., is a visually beautiful piece of penman-ship, but it fails to measure very much that the contemporary critical eye would seek. Though Petrie did record the payments to the estate of the residents of the 109 different farms of Graemeshall and St. Ola parishes, he made no effort to distinguish the manner in which the payments were made, i.e. linen yarn (lint in Scottish parlance), malt, bere, oats, butter, cash, etc. Nor did he compile a separate account that might reveal the purposes of these payments, i.e. rent, Superior Duties, minister's teinds, etc. Finally, it is not evident whether these payments were produced in a single calendar year, although they appear to represent the amount due for the Crop Year 1805. However, the final tally was not made until February 1, 1808.[1] Yet the 1805 Account is useful. The names of all the tenants and their farms are carefully recorded (it is astonishing how many of these same surnames repeat themselves throughout and are still present in the final extant rental in 1887) and the amount and kind of payment rendered. Though farm sizes are not included, from this record we can evaluate the general prosperity of each tenant. It is also worth noting that only three of the tenants at that time were women, one of them being merely listed as Archibald Garrioch's widow.

Subsequent rentals vary considerably in quality, depending upon when they were produced and by whom. David Petrie, Jr.'s accounts have a certain predictability, but are also riddled with inconsistencies that could have driven his superiors mad had they not been so grateful to receive them from him at all. However, none of these rentals adheres to the rigorous accounting principles that were becoming standard for large British businesses. Yet by the 1870s and 1880s that is precisely what this sizeable estate had become.

Bearing in mind that they might lack the exactitude that historians seek, it is nonetheless helpful to examine briefly these surviving estate rentals in order to judge how the Graeme properties fared during the years of agricultural improvement and the subsequent period, until 1887. It must be emphasised that while some of these accounts included all of the Graeme properties, in both Holm and St. Ola parishes, others restricted themselves solely to the lands of Graemeshall estate in Holm parish. Some accounts included the names of the tenants and their farms, while others merely listed the sums of money the estate received. A rough breakdown follows:

Account Book, 1805
    Number of Farms: 109
    Gross Rental: (Holm & St. Ola combined)   £287
    Payments in Kind: Not totalled
    Kelp Sales: Not included[2]

Account Book, 1812
    Number of Farms: 110 (including 6 in St. Ola)
    Gross Rental: Graemeshall   £211
    St. Ola   18
    Total: £229
    Kelp Sales: Not included
    Payments in Kind: Not totalled[3]

Annual State of Accounts, Crop 1827
    Gross Rental: Holm   £499
    St. Ola   40
    Total: £539
    Kelp Sales: £183

Annual State of Accounts, Crop 1828
 Gross Rental: Holm   £505
 St. Ola   41
 Total: £546
 Kelp Sales: £174

Annual State of Accounts, Crop 1829
 Gross Rental: Holm   £477
 St. Ola   39
 Total: £516
 No Kelp Sales

Annual State of Accounts, Crop 1830
 Gross Rental: Holm   £683
 St. Ola   112
 Total: £795
 No Kelp Sales

Annual State of Accounts, Crop 1831
 Gross Rental: Holm   £679
 St. Ola   106
 Total: £785
 Kelp Sales: £132

Annual State of Accounts, Crop 1832
 Gross Rental: Holm   £674
 St. Ola   105
 Total: £779
 No Kelp Sales

Annual State of Accounts, Crop 1833
 Gross Rental: Holm   £674
 St. Ola   105
 Total: £779
 No Kelp Sales

Accumulated Arrears of Rents, 1833
 Total: £332

Annual State of Accounts, Crop 1834
 Gross Rental: Holm   £691
 St. Ola   152
 Total: £843
 No Kelp Sales

List of Arrears of Rents, 1835
      Total Tenants in Arrears: 34
      Total Arrears: £435[4]

List of Arrears of Rents, 1836
      Total Tenants in Arrears: 56
      Total Arrears: £673[5]

Particular Rental of the Estate of Graemeshall . . . for Crop 1840, being the *First* of the *Third Five Years* Endurance of the Tenants Leases . . . Comparing the Rents of the Respective Farms for Crop 1835, with the Rents of Said Farms Respectively for Year and Crop 1840.

Tenants: Holm	64
St. Mary's Village	6
St. Ola	3
Total Tenants:	73

1835
Gross Rental: Holm	£707
St. Ola	104
Total:	£811

1840
Gross Rental: Holm	£775
St. Mary's Village	4
St. Ola	110
Total:	£889

Arrears of Rents, Crop 1840
Number of Tenants:	41
Total:	£415[6]

Rental of the Estate of Graemeshall in the Parishes of Holm and St. Ola, Orkney, Crop Year 1860

Number of Tenants: Holm	62
St. Mary's	7
St. Ola	2
Total Tenants:	71

Gross Rental: Holm   £1334
  St. Ola   290
  Total: £1624

[This was David Petrie's final rental. New leases had gone into effect in the year 1859.][7]

Graemeshall Rental, Crop 1865
  Number of Tenats: Holm   83
  St. Ola   9
  Total Tenants: 92

Gross Rental:Holm   £1349
  St. Ola   300
  Total: £1649[8]

Valuation of the Estate of Graemeshall, 1873
  Number of Farms:Holm parish only.   61
  Gross Rental, Holm parish only.   £1806

[Every farm registered an increase over 1859/1860, some nominally, others nearly doubling.][9]

Rental of Graemeshall Estate, Crop 1880
  Number of Tenants: Holm   78
  St. Ola   15
  Total Tenants: 93

Gross Rental: Holm   £1687
  St. Ola   369
  St. Mary's Village   21
  Misc. (fishing stations, etc.)   33
  Grazings   38
  Total: £2148[10]

Rental for Crop and Year 1887
  Number of Tenants (Graemeshall only)   65
  Gross Rental (Graemeshall only)   £1417[11]

[Every farm had received a rent reduction.]

These rentals succeed in painting a fiscal picture of the estate during the years 1805–1887, though it is a somewhat crude one, composed of broad brushstrokes, with large

portions of the canvas totally untouched by paint. Nonetheless, one can draw several conclusions. The earliest
figures we possess, from the Account Books of 1805 and
1812, represent efforts to track tenants' payments' rather
than to measure the total value of the estate as a whole.
Thus, they do not include the proceeds from the kelp sales,
which were of much greater value at the time than were
agricultural rents.

As the estate managers made a conscious and determined
move toward agricultural improvement, economic concerns and numerical precision assumed greater importance.
As we saw, David Petrie Jr. received an endless stream of
instructions and tirades from John Irving, in the hope that
they would produce a more reliable set of figures with each
year's end, and, as we also saw, these efforts were only
partially successful. From 1827 onward, whenever Petrie
was able to work on them, the annual accounts served as a
much more accurate measure of income and expenditure
than the estate had ever seen in its previous history.
Nonetheless, the gaps are enormous and one can only
wonder how the estate managed to function without them
as a frame of reference. No accounts exist at all for the years
1836–1839, all poor years, and there is no reference in any
of the correspondence indicating their existence. From
1841–1859, we once again face a long stretch of time,
during which improvements were most intense and
singularly successful, when Petrie was unable to concen-
trate his energies on compiling estate statistics. The
'Memorandum' issued by the trustees in March, 1860
expresses the ceaseless frustration they felt in dealing with
Petrie on this matter. Their satisfaction was no greater than
was Irving's.[12] All indications are that the estate accounts
did appear regularly after 1861 with Petrie's departure,
under the factorship of John Armit Bruce. Unfortunately,
only four of them survive in the Orkney County Archives.
However, they are sufficient to provide a rough measure of
the achievements of the estate's agricultural improvement.

The available figures for the years 1827–1840 make it
painfully obvious that the estate did not receive a return

from improvement that was in any way commensurate with the enormous investment that it made. Though it is apparent that the gross rental for 1830 increased by £279 above that of 1829, and was to remain near that level from then on, it can be attributed more to Irving's pressures on Petrie for accelerated payments than to any increased agricultural returns. Furthermore, these figures can be deceptive, for they must be counterbalanced against the dismal increase in accumulated 'Arrears in Rents', for which we possess reliable totals for 1833, 1835, 1836 and 1840. As we saw, these estate investments in improvement occurred just prior to a sustained measurable decline in, and narrowing of, Orkney's economy, and prior to the availability of Parliamentary allocations promoting drainage and roadbuilding in Orkney.[13] Other improving Orkney lairds obtained significant low-interest loans for all phases of the modernisation procedure. One must conclude that during these years, due partly to the earliness of its improving efforts, the estate flirted with bankruptcy, and avoided it by means that are not currently apparent.

Export figures for the entire Orkney economy illustrate the astonishingly poor timing of Graemeshall's improvements. For example, in 1800, Orkney's total exports amounted to £39,677. By 1833, these had risen to only £41,124, truly negligible growth for such a long period. By 1848, Orkney was still exporting goods valued at only £43,736, an unimpressive annual increase of .4% for this 15-year period. Yet in 1861, Orkney exported £156,205 worth of goods, a 20% annual increase for a 13-year period. Thus 1848–1861 were quite clearly years of impressive economic growth. By 1866, Orkney's exports had climbed to £184,380, or a 3.6% annual increase for a five-year period. In 1871, Orkney's exports are recorded as amounting to £242,330, or a 6.3% annual gain for another five-year period. However, by 1885, the total export figures dropped to £218,686, a net loss of £23,644. These numbers were to drop once again in 1886, to £190,827, or a further loss of £27,859.[14] Thus a certain robustness disappeared from the Orkney economic picture, not to reappear for many decades. Thus Graemeshall Estate poured its money into improvement during the years of a regional economic doldrum, thereby precluding a profitable conclusion. Orkney's economy was to enjoy a take-off only during the latter 1840s. For example, by 1848, Orkney was exporting 8,000 live beef cattle per year and the economy entered decades of strong growth.[15]

Although the Laird of Graemeshall was deeply mired in personal debt, the trustees were successful in keeping these obligations separate from the Orkney estate accounts. They were also able to fund his debts through a variety of schemes tied more closely to the fortunes of the family than to the estate. By 1840 there was a slight increase in the gross rental of the estate, but an even greater decline took place in the accumulated arrears of rents, from £683 in 1836 to £415 in 1840. All correspondence during the 1840s reflects a continuing slide in this once menacing deficit, and a notable improvement in the fortunes of the estate. On the other hand, available sources reveal that the estate was compelled to sell off a substantial acreage. The sale in 1848 of 1,500 acres of the former commons to Thomas Traill, Esq., of Holland has already been mentioned. A. C. O'Dell, reporting on the 15 Orkney heritors who owned 71.2% of the land in the Islands during 1872, noted that the Graemeshall estate possessed 6,444 acres, considerably less than the more than 13,000 recorded in 1831.[16] These substantial land sales, all of which occurred during a period when estate records are sparse, would have improved the fiscal condition of Graemeshall. It is also entirely possible that they could have served to eliminate the laird's substantial debts.

The other heritors in Orkney who were venturesome in improving their lands did not begin their efforts until the 1840s, just before the agricultural boom in the latter years of that decade. As W. P. L. Thomson has noted: 'Under the stimulus of greatly improved cattle prices Orkney entered a period of intense and sustained growth (1848–1871) which entirely transformed the Orkney economy, its landscape, and the way of life of its inhabitants'.[17] The Graeme properties, having both pioneered and survived, were in an excellent position to profit from this economic surge. Well-situated for agricultural export, with some of the very best cattle country in the Islands, under the continuing guidance of David Petrie, Jr., a man widely regarded as a skilled and adept practitioner, Graemeshall was known as a vanguard estate.[18]

David Petrie's final rental before his dismissal, for the crop year 1860, reflected the significant strengthening of the economic status of the Graeme properties. The total value of the rentals had nearly doubled since 1840 and the tenants' arrears of rents, since they are not mentioned, had most likely vanished. It is unfortunate that no estate correspondence has survived from this period to add to the picture. However, there is no doubt that the troubled times were over. Improvements continued over the next twenty years, but they were much less dramatic in scale. Pringle, writing in 1874, discussed the pioneering improvement experience in Holm parish, but he also makes the reader aware that Graemeshall estate was not advancing as rapidly as were other Orkney properties.[19] In examining the annual valuation of the rentals of Holm parish from 1855 until 1884, we are able to see a total increase from £1,095 to £2,924. For this 29-year period, Holm rentals grew a total of 167%, or increased 2½ times, but at an annual rate of only 5.7%.[20] Allowing that Holm represented only a portion of the Graeme properties, and acknowledging the fact that much Holm property had been sold, these results are not overly impressive. Perhaps the guiding hands of the quirky and quixotic David Petrie, Jr., were sorely missed and his skills not easily duplicated.

Accompanying the 1873 Valuation of the Estate is a handwritten report, farm by farm, for the Holm parish property. These include numerous comments on the state of cultivation, conditions of the soil, etc., on each of the 61 rental properties on the estate. This unsigned document, written in a different hand from that on the rental, reveals an uneven movement toward improvement among the different farms and tenants on the estate, at a time that represented the peak of agricultural prosperity. A few of the farms were deemed worthy of the terse comment 'well farmed' or 'very well farmed'. Some earned praise, but with specific recommendations, i.e. 'requires drains and regular manure', or 'requires water course cleared', and in the case of the 42-acre farm of Ferryhouse, 'this farm is much exposed to sea blast, is very poor, needs more manure'. Other farms earned the opprobrium of the observer, i.e. 'not well-farmed', 'badly farmed', 'poorly worked', or 'not well cultivated'. In the eyes of this unknown observer, most of the farms on the estate fell in-between, earning such comments as 'farmed fairly'. In spite of all the years of recommendations by John Irving, Graemeshall in 1873 was still primarily an estate of small farms, several of no more than 11 to 16 acres, earning very modest rents. The majority of the farms were in the 30–60 acre range, while the largest farms, Cornquoy at 102 acres, Vigga at 104 acres, Graemeshall at 154 acres or Greenwall at 195 acres, were still not colossal farming enterprises when measured by the standards of the Scottish mainland at that time.[21] Thus the realisation of Irving's most cherished schemes was never more than partial.

During the first years of agricultural improvement, 1828–1834, the estate spent a sum greater than £50 erecting new farm steadings on seven different properties. Of these farms, only three fell into the 'well-farmed' category of 1873. One of them, Gutterpool, was described as 'poorly farmed', while Northouse earned the description 'not well farmed'. The other two were described as 'farmed fairly'. On the other hand, several farms on which the estate had lavished no capital improvements at all during this earlier period were designated as models of cultivation and earned praise.[22] This comparison suggests that these expenditures were not particularly well-directed, or, even worse, that much of the money was prematurely spent and thus simply wasted. The character and skills of the sitting tenant counted for more than did these estate expenditures.

In 1873, Alexander Malcolm Sutherland Graeme (1845–1908), the only heir of the Laird of Graemeshall, married

Margaret-Isabel Neale, daughter of the noted hymnologist and Warden of Sackville College, East Grinstead, Sussex, Dr. John Mason Neale, D. D. The marriage contract revealed that the bride was from a family so wealthy that the fortunes of the estate were transformed and that Malcolm Graeme, following his years of training as a naval officer, was freed from the worries of ever having to adopt a profession.[23] The marriage also permitted the groom to fulfill a dream he had ever since his first visit, in 1865, as a 20-year-old to his family estate. In 1874 he began the elaborate construction of the new and larger mansion of Graemeshall, which was completed by summer, 1876. There was no evident concern about the costs of this venture and he spared no expense. Malcolm, his wife and infant daughter moved into the spacious new dwelling and remained there much of each year, although they also maintained their family property at St. Leonard's-by-the-Sea on the English Channel. Thus, for the first time in 90 years, a member of the Graeme family was now resident on the ancestral estate. On March 7, 1877, the recently widowed 'old laird', Alexander Sutherland Graeme, made his third and final visit to the estate, which he had not seen for 43 years.[24] One can only regret that we do not possess a journal account of his impressions of the changes that had taken place in the parish during this lengthy period.

Readers of the *Orcadian* for the 1860s, 1870s and 1880s will see many references noting the active presence of Alexander Malcolm Sutherland Graeme and his wife in the affairs of the family property in Orkney. He and his family undoubtedly added a welcome element of sociability to the parish that had been lacking since the previous century. For example, in November, 1868 he hosted the Harvest Home festival in Holm, at which 390 people were present in Thomas Traill's barn, the largest structure in the parish at the time. It is notable that Graeme was evidently pleased to toast his 'particularly good friend, Mr. David Petrie', then the oldest tenant on the estate. Graeme reminded all present that evening that Petrie had been factor for many years and that he 'respected him as much as if he had been factor now'. Petrie himself addressed the crowd and was warmly received.[25] Again, in 1883, Mr. Graeme and his wife entertained over 350 tenants and their families at the laird's expense. These festivities were held in the New Drill Hall for the Holm company of the Orkney Volunteers, erected by the estate, in the village of St. Mary's. Mr. Graeme and the factor, John Armit Bruce, spoke at the gathering, after which Mrs. Graeme led the tenantry in a round of song. The *Orcadian* reported that the daughter of a hymnologist 'sang beautifully'.[26] On other occasions, Alexander Malcolm Sutherland Graeme chaired the Orkney Agricultural Society's annual cattle show, but, even more frequently, he actively represented landlord and propertied interests throughout Orkney during the 1880s when they appeared to be threatened.[27] While resident in England, Graeme frequently used his time to earnestly campaign on behalf of Conservative Party causes, serving as speaker for numerous gatherings.

At the moment that Malcolm Sutherland Graeme ordered the rebuilding of the family estate house, the Orkneys were in the vanguard of agricultural prosperity in the north of Scotland. In the words of A. C. O'Dell:

> Primarily as a result of the reclamation improvements in Orcadian agriculture, Orkney changed from the position of one of the most backward counties to that of the most agriculturally advanced in Scotland north of the Highland line.[28]

But it was not merely the quality and profitability of Orkney agriculture that had changed. So had the primary commodities that the Islands produced. A traditional, but decidedly marginal, grain-producing region had successfully made the transition to raising and transporting livestock, a capital-intensive product, for export to the mainland market. Pringle noted that Orkney beef cattle were widely regarded as 'great thrivers' when taken south, free from such contagious maladies as pleuro-pneumonia and foot and mouth disease. A sea voyage by steamship from Kirkwall to Aberdeen would usually last no more than ten hours, ensuring that cattle arrived in a very fresh state, ready to begin the fattening-up process. Pringle estimated that in 1871 Orkney was home to 22,830 head of cattle, as well as 26,978 sheep. At that moment he doubted that the Islands had yet reached their potential, since great tracts of reclaimable wasteland still remained. He speculated that Orkney could well see a doubling of its livestock numbers within the next fifteen or twenty years.[29] In 1887, John Watson observed that Orkney was raising 25,726 cattle and 33,067 sheep, although by then the Islands' agriculture was already past its peak. In that year, the 8,194 head of exported live cattle earned £90,134.[30] Orkney also exported great quantities of live sheep and pigs, as well as potatoes and eggs, during the 1870s.[31] As Ernest Marwick observed: 'Few Scottish counties have a greater proportion of arable land than Orkney, which is why our agriculture, once unshackled, prospered so greatly'. Marwick calculated that the proportion of arable to total land area in Scotland as a whole in the year 1881 was 18.83%. For Shetland the proportion was 4.72% but for Orkney it was at that time an impressive 36.51%.[32]

During the 1870s British agriculture suffered the devastating effects of a downturn caused in part by a free trade movement that eventually led to the import of cheaper grain from such overseas outposts of European settlement as North America, Argentina and Australia. However, in Orkney, with its livestock-based economy, the adverse effects were delayed for a decade. The 1880 Rental for the Graemeshall Estate, for example, reflected this continuing profitability, though no dramatic improvements were recorded over 1874. However, the Rental for Crop and Year 1887 provides the clearest intimation that the good times for the estate were over by then. Readers of the *Orcadian* during the 1880s can sense a depressed and ominous mood, particularly if they choose to read the steady stream of statistics describing agricultural imports into such large cities as Glasgow, Birmingham or Liverpool. It was becoming strikingly evident that the British were choosing to rely for their food sources on those parts of the world where products could be grown in greatest quantity for the lowest costs. Thus, the greatly diminished shipping costs that permitted Orcadian products to reach the British mainland were simultaneously permitting agricultural products from North America, Argentina, Australia and New Zealand to drive some British commodities from their home markets.

During the 1880s parts of the Highlands and especially the Isle of Skye experienced rural disturbances similar to those of Ireland, though not nearly as intense. To defuse the situation, the Gladstone government directed the Napier Commission (1883) to take testimony within the crofting counties of the Highlands and Islands and secure concessions on behalf of the peasants from the landed classes. The Commission's Report led to the Crofters' Act of 1886, which called for an investigation, employing further oral testimony, into conditions in the crofting counties of Scotland.[33] This represented an unusual exercise of state power in late nineteenth-century Britain and a major departure from the principles of *laissez-faire* economics.[34]

The Crofters' Commission visit to Orkney in 1888 occurred at a time when the entire notion of landed property rights in Scotland was coming under challenge. There is no greater indicator that the balance of social forces in Britain was shifting against the old landed elites than the decisions rendered by this government commission. The Commission decidedly favoured the claims of the tenants over those of the local lairds. Of the 443 individual cases heard in Orkney, 30 came from residents of Graemeshall estate, with another ten presented by Mr. Graeme's St. Ola tenants. The testimony, taken in Kirkwall Court House during September 18, 19 and 22, 1888, is quite valuable in that it provides us with a rare insight into the thinking of the tenant and crofter class of Orkney. Mr. Andrew Thomson acted as agent for the crofters, but each claimant offered personal testimony of the grievances at issue. Sheriff David Brand chaired the proceedings, while Alexander Malcolm Sutherland

Graeme represented his father, now enfeebled, for both the Graemeshall and St. Ola properties. A clerk recorded the resulting dialogue.[35]

The absence of the rancour and antagonism that dominated some of these hearings in Orkney (particularly on the island of Rousay) is most notable.[36] The tenants were free to describe their personal circumstances as fully as they wished and at no time did any tenant express a negative feeling toward the proprietor. Nor did Mr. Graeme attempt to vilify any of the tenants. At the onset of the hearings Graeme was eager for the record to reflect that his relationship with the tenants and crofters 'had hitherto been of a most cordial and kindly character'. Thomson hastened to concur with this assessment.[37]

In general, Graeme defended the rights and privileges of private property and the sanctity of contract, though one senses that the lack of vigour in his presentation indicates that he saw he was confronting a historical tide flowing against him. The tenants' and crofters' complaints tended to follow a pattern: their rents were too high for current market conditions; they were not properly compensated by the laird for such permanent improvements as breaking in new land, drains and ditches, and farm buildings; and loss of access to the former common lands (in effect, denied them in 1857, in most cases to their fathers or other relatives). Finally, several of the tenants refer to the steady decline of the prices received for agricultural products.

However, it is worthy of note that not a single tenant chose to offer a fundamental challenge to Graeme's right to own the land, to collect rents from them, or to exercise his many other privileges. The level of rural radicalism so prevalent in Ireland and Skye found no echo among these Orkney farmfolk. Nor is there any indication that these tenants elevated their personal grievances to the higher level of abstract political principle. The old hegemony of the laird was being undermined, but it was as yet far from being overthrown.

In general, the tenants and sub-tenants who presented themselves before the Commission, as demanded by the requirements, tended to be of the poorer sort. There were a goodly number whose annual rental amounted to no more than £3–6, but who had accumulated arrears of double or treble that amount during the previous few years of economic crisis. This was to be very much expected. A few of these witnesses were quite marginal examples. For example, Mary Laughton of Mutton Hall lived on 3½ acres of arable land and a 3¼ of outrun. Her annual rent was £3. She was a sub-tenant of a relative, but she and her sister were also day labourers for several other farmers, who she said materially assisted them. The Commission reduced her rent to £2 annually.[38] Another sub-tenant, William Sinclair of Skolls, farmed eight acres of arable for £3 17s 6d a year. He had not paid his rent in six years and was deeply in arrears. He did assert that he had reclaimed five acres of moorland and had erected buildings valued at £58. When he became a resident in 1853 he was free to graze his stock on the common lands, but now he was deprived of that right. Graeme said that the man could sit rent-free: that he had no wish to remove him.[39]

However, there were several tenants of more substantial means who barely qualified as actual crofters, men such as James Sclater of Midhouse, whose farm consisted of 50 acres of arable with 20 acres of outrun. An annual rental of £29 would classify him as a mid-sized farmer in Orkney. Yet Sclater was £25 in arrears and requested relief. The Commission reduced his rent to £24 14s and cancelled £6 17s of his arrears. In the appendix to the 1874 rental, Sclater's croft had been listed as 'well-farmed'.[40] Or one could use the example of David Inkster of Hunclett, who farmed 70 acres of arable along with 30 acres of outrun and who paid an annual rental of £25 15s. In 1888, Inkster's arrears had grown to £92 15s. Graeme described him in the hearings as 'a most industrious tenant' and said that he 'had a high opinion of him'. The Commission reduced Inkster's rental to £18 15s and cancelled £27 of his arrears. In 1874, Inkster's property had been described as 'fairly farmed'.[41] As a final example of a mid-size farmer newly in trouble there was Robert Tait of Backakelday, who paid a rental of

£29 for 54 acres of arable and 8 acres of outrun. He had reclaimed 37 acres of heath and built all structures on the croft. Yet his arrears, which had climbed to over £61, were partly due to the loss of many of his cattle through 'seagust', to which his property was vulnerable. The Commission reduced Tait's rent to £21 14s and cancelled over £16 of his arrears. These few examples should indicate that Graemeshall was facing a systemic problem of significant dimensions.

The loss of access to the common lands in 1857 was still a burning memory in the minds of several tenants. Although only six of the 30 tenants from Graemeshall who had petitioned the Commission explicitly complained about this loss, there can be little doubt that the subject was on the minds of many others. We must bear in mind that it took a poor person a great deal of courage to raise such a subject in a public forum, in the presence of the laird and the County Sheriff. Other tenants plainly had the same subject in mind when they asserted that their farms were not viable, under present arrangements. For example, William Louttit of Woodstock had become a tenant in 1855. Before then he had lived as a squatter on the bare hillside. He complained that he had been denied grazing rights on the Commons in 1857, 'along with the other tenants in Holm'. Georgina Eunson of Hower, who farmed 57 acres of arable and one of outrun, had been a tenant for four years, ever since her husband's death. He had been there for 19 years previously and, before then, her father-in-law had been a tenant for 23 years. During these 46 years of tenancy, her family had reclaimed 38 acres of hillside, yet had been denied grazing privileges on the Commons in 1857. Another tenant, David Esson of Chackhole, had held a lease for eight years. However, his uncle was there for 48 years before him. Yet he reported that in 1857 his uncle had been 'deprived of grazing on the skaws of Greenwall'. Thus, customary rights that had been legally lost for 40 years, and in practice, lost for 31 years, were very much in the minds of the tenants of Graemeshall in 1888. If E. P. Thompson's findings in England are valid for Orkney, then the loss of these customary rights affected their ability to make a go of their small farms. Thompson argued that the costs might have been 'most significant for the livelihood of the poor and the marginal people'. The Common rights, now regarded in formal law as usurpations, had often provided the margin for a sustainable existence for these hill crofters and cottars.[42]

It is significant that none of the largest tenants of Graeme's lands made his voice heard in these proceedings. For example, the name of James Heddle of Greenwall, whose annual rent was greater than £151, was not before the Commission, nor was that of James Oddie of Cornquoy, who paid more than £58 rental, nor do we discover a petition from Thomas Anderson of Lingro in the parish of St. Ola, whose rental was £188 per year.[43] Either the agricultural depression had not worked its way that far up the scale, or these larger farmers' rents prohibited them from qualifying as crofters before the Commission.[44]

The Commission's decisions resulted in a total rent reduction on the estate of about 27%, with about 49% of the arrears being cancelled outright. Alexander Malcolm Sutherland Graeme responded with pique and cynicism, but not outrage. He corrected several insinuations and impressions that had crept into the argument and wryly noted that the total value of all the dwellings and structures that tenants claimed to have erected on their own amounted to £2,657, an amount equivalent to eleven years' rental on these particular properties. He also hastened to remind the Commission that the landlord owned the land that was being improved and therefore deserved a good share of the benefits from that improvement. On a more philosophical note, he did claim to recognise that certain formerly moral rights that tenants associated with improvement were, in fact, rapidly becoming rights recognised by the laws of the Kingdom.[45]

Thus, the London government bought rural peace in Scotland, at the expense of an already declining landed élite.[46] The crofters were afforded a measure of protection that permitted them to survive as a class, though nothing was done to solve the twin problems of over-population and land-hunger in Orkney. Emigration from the Islands remained a social fact for decades to come. The lairds were, however, in the process of losing their economic under-pinnings along with parts of their estates. The *Orcadian* understood this changing state of affairs when, in 1887, it observed that 'In future the laird is to be a mere rent-collecting machine, and the rent to be paid is not to be measured by the mercenary spirit of the receiver'.[47] In other words, when a landlord no longer has it in his power to fix rents, can he, in fact, remain lord of the land? Thus the 1880s represented a decisive watershed in Orkney's history: they heralded the beginning of the end of well over three centuries of landlord domination of these Islands.[48]

Notes

1   OCA, D5/12/5.
2   Ibid., D5/3/8.
3   Ibid., D5/12/6.
4   Ibid., D5/4/2.
5   Ibid., D5/4/4.
6   Ibid., D5/46/9.
7   Ibid.
8   Ibid.
9   Ibid., D5/44/4.
10 Ibid., D5/46/9.
11 Ibid.
12 Ibid., D5/4/7.
13 Thomson, *History of Orkney*, pp. 222–228; O'Dell, pp. 199–200.
14 *Orkney Herald*, October 31, 1888.
15 Thomson, *History of Orkney*, p. 228.
16 O'Dell, p. 200.
17 Thomson, *History of Orkney*, p. 226. See also Pringle.
18 O'Dell, p. 210.
19 Pringle, pp. 10 and 55–56.
20 *Orcadian*, 1855–1885.
21 OCA, D5/44/4.
22 Ibid., D5/12/7.
23 Ibid., D5/4/7. '*Patias Amicis*', p. 50, gives January 25, 1874, as the date of the wedding, which took place in Brighton. Though

his service in the navy was fairly brief, Lieutenant Sutherland Graeme sailed aboard H.M.S. *Topaz* to California, the West Indies and South America.

24 *Pateas Amicis*, pp. 40–52.

25 *Orcadian*, November 10, 1868. We should bear in mind that at the moment that Petrie was being honoured and cheered, he was also the subject of eviction proceedings in the Sheriff Court in Kirkwall.

26 *Orcadian*, January 20, 1883.

27 *Orcadian*. August 18, 1883, August 25, 1883. Unlike his father, whose death was all but ignored by the Orkney newspapers, Alexander Malcolm's death, at the age of 63, was extensively noted, and regretted, in lengthy obituaries. Both the *Orcadian*, February 8, 1908, and the *Orkney Herald*, February 5, 1908, described his commanding and influential presence in the parish, as well as in the county: he served as Deputy Lieutenant, Commissioner of Supply, Justice of the Peace, Member of the Piers and Harbour Commission, and Member of the County Council. In Holm parish, Graeme achieved membership in the Parish Council, School Board and was an officer of the Orkney Artillery Volunteers. He was also a member of St. Olaf's Episcopalian Church, Kirkwall, and, for a long time, a Church Warden, Manager, and Lay Elector. He left a widow, one daughter and four sons.

28 O'Dell, p. 202.

29 Pringle, pp. 60–61.

30 John Watson, *Tenancy and Ownership* (London, 1889) p. 45; *Orkney Herald*, October 31, 1888.

31 O'Dell, pp. 250–251. Orkney egg exports increased from £2,500 per annum in 1861 to £40,560 for the year 1886. *Orkney Herald*. October 31, 1888.

32 E. Marwick, *Orcadian*, May 13, 1954.

33 Thomson, *History of Orkney*, p. 229.

34 James Hunter, *The Making of the Crofting Community* (Edinburgh, 1976), p. 162.

35 W. R. Macintosh, *The Orkney Crofters: Their Evidence and Statements by Agents, as given before the Crofters' Commission* (Kirkwall, 1889), pp. 206–225 and 265–271.

36 For the conflict in Rousay, see the excellent study by William P. L. Thomson, *The Little General and the Rousay Crofters: Crisis and Conflict on an Orkney Estate* (Edinburgh, 1981).

37 *Ibid.*, p. 208.

38 *Ibid.*, p. 212.

39 *Ibid.*, p. 213.

40 *Ibid.*, p. 213; OCA. D5/44/4.

41 Macintosh, p. 217; OCA. D5/44/4.

42 E. P. Thompson, *Customs in Common*, pp. 100–101.

43 OCA, D5/46/9.

44 A crofter's annual rental could be no greater than £30: Thomson, *History of Orkney*. p. 260. James Hunter defines a crofter as 'a small tenant of land with or without a lease, who finds in the cultivation of his holding a material portion of his occupation, earnings and sustenance . . .' However, to meet the needs of his family fully, the crofter also required some means of ancillary employment. Hunter, p. 3.

45 Macintosh, p. 222.

46 Thomson, *History of Orkney*, pp. 228–229.

47 *Orcadian*, January 29, 1887.

48 W. P. L. Thomson discusses a subject that, unfortunately, must remain beyond the scope of this study, i.e. the gradual but steady break-up of these estates in the years following the First World War. Many of the estate houses had become mere relics by then, deprived for decades of the investment necessary for their maintenance. Thomson, *History of Orkney*, pp. 241–242.

Conclusion

When historians study large processes, they often lose sight of the decisive role of human agency among the factors influencing the eventual outcome. This study of a particular example of agricultural change directs the inquiry precisely in that direction. However, all too often the raw material for this type of historical research in Scottish rural societies—family and estate papers deposited in county archives or in private hands—remains unexplored. Admittedly, unpublished sources are difficult to use (or at times even to read), but they frequently yield unexpected and fascinating results. The particulars that emerge provide much of the texture that the broader picture frequently lacks. If necessary, they can be supplemented by the secondary literature as well as centralised archival records, such as in the Scottish Record Office. Fortunately for Scottish historians, David Moody's recent guidebook points to several paths through this often impenetrable thicket.[1]

Since agricultural improvement is usually depicted as an inexorable process, a local study such as this suggests that unless timing and execution were properly coordinated, agricultural improvements were a perilous, and potentially fatal, undertaking for an estate. As we have seen, a premature improving effort, financed largely by estate and family sources, one that encountered substantial tenant resistance and non-cooperation, at least in its ill-fated early phase, could postpone for decades the earning of profit. There is little doubt that if Graemeshall had delayed its modernisation for a couple of decades, if it had undertaken it on a more modest scale, if it had been able to avail itself of thousands of pounds of low-interest government loans for drainage and roadbuilding, had it been able to market its produce more readily at an earlier date, the outcome would have been more favourable. But the estate's timing was poor, the initial expenditures were far too high, the leadership was at cross-purposes with itself, all at a moment when Orkney's export markets were languishing. Indeed, most of the improvement efforts and expenditures on this estate were made prior to Orkney's significant export growth, which did not begin until about 1848.[2] Finally, since Orkney was an island community with its own local traditions, farm sizes remained so small, and the land so fragmented, that economies of scale were unlikely to be realised. Fundamentally, it was the preposterous failure to appreciate the difficulties associated with insularity and relative isolation that led directly to decades of crisis for these properties.

Orkney's Age of Improvement, 1848–1883, roughly corresponded to what others characterise as the age of 'Victorian High Farming'. Howard Newby recently described this as 'a high input, high output system of intensive farming', which also conveyed high status as one of its rewards.[3] In addition, he demonstrated that 'High Farming' was a distinct system that employed at its very core 'an essential change in the access to, and rights over, property'. As a result, property was now 'freed of any social obligations which had hitherto rested upon its ownership . . .' The improving proprietor was seen to have free play with respect to the uses of the land, free from any constraints imposed by local custom.[4] On the whole, however, Newby depicted the entire British 'High Farming' experience as a strategic miscalculation and misdirection of resources. In his view, such expenditures could only be recouped if rents remained very high for many decades, an unlikely prospect given the ever-present probability of an economic downturn. In Newby's assessment, in an age of free trade, with a national commercial policy that left agriculture unprotected from low-cost overseas competition, higher returns would have been achieved if the money had been invested in commerce and industry.[5] If Newby's assessment of English agriculture is correct, how would his formulation fare if applied to islands in the north of Scotland?

Though livestock prices dropped less rapidly than did those for grain, British agriculture was to remain in a state of chronic depression from 1875 until 1939, except for the brief interruption of the Great War.

With this in mind, it is difficult to justify, with a historian's vision derived from twenty-twenty hindsight, the efforts that were made to modernise the estate of Graemeshall during the years 1827–1888. Though our economic data are certainly far from complete, the records indicate that neither the estate nor the proprietor earned any profit from improvement from 1828 until 1848. Good money was repeatedly thrown after bad during this generation of improvement. Indeed, for a portion of this period, the estate appeared to be undergoing a subsistence crisis. Alexander Sutherland Graeme, a chronically absentee laird, plunged himself into economic despair and continued to require repeated rescue by the trustees of the family fortune, while David Petrie, Jr., got into severe difficulties with his own accounts by the late 1840s. Yet Graemeshall estate did enjoy quite notable and impressive economic prosperity during the 1850s, 1860s and 1870s, as measured by the steady rise in the total rental, though it is impossible to determine whether the final figures would have compensated for the earlier full generation of losses. Nor do we know for certain whether the tenants were able to benefit from such an early start. The record strongly suggests that a good many did not. During the 1830s they found it impossible to share in the optimism of the proprietor about the prospects for success and they repeatedly resisted the changes that they felt were being imposed from above. Plainly, for many of them the initial uncertainty was intolerable. They thus focused on what they had lost during improvement. The growing lack of access to the common lands, when coupled with the application of the stringent terms of the new leases, greatly impinged on their customary freedoms. It is regrettable that the records are unable to penetrate the anonymity of so many of the inhabitants of the estate. Nonetheless, E. P. Thompson has astutely observed, in a manner applicable to events in Orkney, that during the process of improvement:

> Property must be made palpable, loosed for the market from its uses and from its social situation, made capable of being hedged and fenced, of being owned quite independently of any grid of custom or mutuality.[6]

There can be no doubt that the unrestrained application of market forces proved beneficial only to a small portion of this rural population.

During the age of improvement many tenants began to leave their farms, and a small number were removed for non-payment of rent. The surviving rentals inform us that the number of tenants was substantially reduced during the period from 1805 (109 tenants) until 1840 (73 tenants), but these numbers were to rise once again (93 tenants in 1880) as the commons were brought under cultivation and new farms were carved from the heather. The total acreage being cultivated steadily increased. Unfortunately, we have no reliable information on the several hundred labourers and cottars resident on the property, though if trends observable elsewhere hold true of this estate, there was less work available to them after the initial preparations for improvement—ditching, draining and roadbuilding— were completed. William P. L. Thomson feels that for Orkney in general this social class enjoyed little security of tenure and that 'the great majority of crofters were seriously under-employed'.[7] The population figures for the parish of Holm offer little clue as to the specific employment of most of the inhabitants. Between 1801 and 1851, the parish population varied slightly, between 871 and 749. It then rose rapidly until it peaked in 1881 at a total of 1091 people, just in time for a new economic crisis. After this, it steadily dropped. In 1981, only 558 people lived in Holm.[8] Many of these poorer rural people became redundant all over Scotland at this time and thousands were compelled to either emigrate or move south in search of employment. By the 1850s a government-operated emigration office, located in Kirkwall, routinely facilitated overseas migration of Orcadians to the British Empire and the Dominions.[9]

The much-vaunted Age of Improvement, when viewed from the particular experience of the Graemeshall estate in the Orkneys, presents a picture of muddled direction, a mixture of successful and failed initiatives, not to mention a rather tortured complexity. The triumphal march into modernity and certain profit proved to be both chimerical and transitory.

Notes

1 David Moody, *Scottish Local History: An Introductory Guide* (London, 1986).
2 William P. L. Thomson, *The Little General . . .*, p. 30. For the finest general picture of Orkney's 'Age of Improvement', see Chapter 4 of that book.
3 Howard Newby, *Country Life . . .*, p. 55.
4 *Ibid.*, pp. 12–14.
5 *Ibid.*, p. 70.
6 E. P. Thompson, 'The Grid of Inheritance: A Comment.' in Jack Goody, Joan Thirsk, and E. P. Thompson (eds) *Family and Inheritance: Rural Society in Western Europe*. Cambridge: 1976. pp. 328–360.
7 Thomson, *History of Orkney*, p. 224.
8 Robert Barclay, *Population of Orkney* (Kirkwall, 1961), p. 14.
9 *Orcadian*, vol. ii, No. 14, 10 November, 1855.

Glossary

Bere   Also known as bear. A primitive, hardy, four-rowed barley, of inferior yield, commonly grown throughout Scotland. Ordinary barley has only two rows.

Brecklands   Also referred to as breaklands, muirs, moors, mosses or marches. Unimproved land, mostly still under heather. Primarily lands that once belonged to the commonty.

Crofter   Holder of a croft, i.e. a small portion of arable land, held directly from the laird. Usually insufficient for the support of a family. Defined by the Crofters Holding Act of 1886 as a tenant paying less than £30 per annum.

Factor   Person employed by landowner to manage the estate and to collect rent payments.

Feu   Feudal property holding.

Laird   Proprietor of a tenanted estate.

Outrun   Land that was, as yet, unimproved. Primarily useful for rough grazing.

Planking   The consolidation of several scattered rigs into a single block, capable of being farmed by one person.

Runrig   A traditional Scottish system of landholding in which land was distributed in a series of scattered strips, or ridges. These rigs were frequently intermingled with those of other tenants, commonly leading to disputes.

Teind   Church tax or tithe, based on the tenth part of the annual produce of the land.

Bibliography

Orkney county archives

MANUSCRIPT RECORDS

Sutherland Graeme Papers D5.
Watt of Breckness Papers, D3.
Taylor Papers, D9.
Sheriff Court Papers, SC.

Newspapers

The Orcadian, 1854-present.
The Orkney Herald, 1860–1960.
The Scotsman.

PRINTED RECORDS

O'Dell, A. C., *The Land of Britain: The Report of the Land Utilisation Survey of Britain*, Part 4, *Orkney*. London: 1939.
Poor Law Inquiry Commission for Scotland, Orkney. Edinburgh: 1843.
Report of Her Majesty's Commissioners appointed to enquire into the conditions of the crofters and cottars in the Highlands and Islands of Scotland. London: 1884.
Report to the Board of Agriculture for Scotland on Home Industries in the Highlands and Islands. London: 1914.

SECONDARY WORKS

General

Jones, Eric L., 'Afterword', in Parker, W. N. and Jones, E. L. (eds.), *European Peasants and their Markets*. Princeton: 1975.

Thompson, E. P., 'The Grid of Inheritance: a Comment', in Goody, Jack, Thirsk, Joan, and Thompson, E. P. (eds.), *Family and Inheritance: Rural Society in Western Europe*. Cambridge: 1976.

Thompson, E. P., *Customs in Common: Studies in Traditional Popular Culture*. New York: 1993.

Great Britain

Berg, Maxine, *The Age of Manufactures: Industry, Innovation and Work in Britain, 1700–1820*. New York: 1985.

Burke's Landed Gentry. London: 1898.

Colley, Linda, *Britons: Forging the Nation, 1707–1837*. New Haven: 1992.

Howkins, Alun, *Reshaping Rural England: A Social History, 1850–1925*. London: 1991.

Mingay, G. E., *The Gentry: The Rise and Fall of a Ruling Class*. London: 1976.

Mingay, G. E., *The Agricultural Revolution: Changes in Agriculture, 1650–1880*. London: 1977.

Mingay, G. E. (ed.), *The Victorian Countryside*, Vols. 1 & 2. London: 1981.

Newby, Howard, *County Life: A Social History of Rural England*. London: 1987.

Royle, Edward, *Modern Britain: A Social History, 1750–1985*. London: 1987.

Spring, David, *The English Landed Estate in the Nineteenth Century: Its Administration*. Baltimore: 1963.

Thompson, F. M. L., *English Landed Society in the Nineteenth Century*. London: 1963.

Scotland

Brown, Callum G., 'Religion and Social Change', in Devine, T. E. & Mitchison, Rosalind (eds.), *People and Society in Scotland, 1740–1830*, Vol. 1. Edinburgh: 1988.

Campbell, R. H., 'The Scottish Improvers and the Course of Agrarian Change in the Eighteenth Century', in

Cullen, L. M. & Smout, T. C. (eds.), *Comparative Aspects of Scottish and Irish Economic and Social History, 1600–1800*. Edinburgh: 1976.

Catford, E. F., *Edinburgh: The Story of a City*. Edinburgh: 1975.

Fenton, Alexander, *Scottish Country Life*. Edinburgh: 1976.

Fry, Michael, *Patronage and Principle: A Political History of Modern Scotland*. Aberdeen: 1987.

Grierson, H. J. C., (ed.), *The Letters of Sir Walter Scott*. London: 1832.

Handley, J. E., *Scottish Farming in the Eighteenth Century*. London: 1953.

Handley, J. E., *The Agricultural Revolution in Scotland*. Glasgow: 1963.

Hunter, James, *The Making of the Crofting Community*. Edinburgh: 1976.

Karras, Alan L., *Sojourners in the Sun: Scottish Migrants in Jamaica and the Chesapeake, 1740–1800*. Ithaca: 1992.

Knox, Susan A., *The Making of the Shetland Landscape*. Edinburgh: 1985.

Lenman, Bruce, *Integration, Enlightenment, and Industrialization: 1746–1832*. Toronto: 1981.

Moody, David, *Scottish Local History: An Introductory Guide*. London: 1986.

Morris, R. J., 'Scotland, 1830–1914: The Making of a Nation within a Nation', in Fraser, W. Hamish & Morris, R. J. (eds.), *People and Society in Scotland*, Vol. II. Edinburgh: 1990.

Parry, M. L., 'Changes in the Extent of Improved Farmland', in Parry, M. L. & Slater, T. R. (eds.), *The Making of the Scottish Countryside*. Edinburgh: 1980.

Shaw, F. J., *The Northern and Western Isles of Scotland*. Edinburgh: 1980.

Sinclair, Sir John, *General View of the Agriculture of the Northern Counties and Islands of Scotland*. London: 1795.

Smith, Hance D., *Shetland Life and Trade, 1550–1914*. Edinburgh: 1984.

Smout, T. C., *A History of the Scottish People: 1560–1830*. New York: 1969.

Smout, T. C., *A Century of the Scottish People: 1830–1950*. London: 1986.

Smout, T. C., 'Scottish Landowners and Economic Growth, 1650–1850', *Scottish Journal of Political Economy*, II, pp. 218–234. 1964.

Symon, J. A., *Scottish Farming Past and Present*. Edinburgh: 1959.

Whittington, G. & Whyte, I. D. (eds), *An Historical Geography of Scotland*. London: 1983.

Whyte, I. D., 'George Dundas of Dundas: The Context of an Early Eighteenth Century Scottish Improving Landowner', *Scottish Historical Review*. 1981.

Orkney

Barclay, Robert, *The Population of Orkney*. Kirkwall, 1961.

Barry, George, *The History of the Orkney Islands* (2nd Edition). Kirkwall: 1867.

Cormack, Alexander & Ann, *The Days of Orkney Steam*. Kirkwall: 1971.

Fenton, Alexander, *The Northern Isles: Orkney and Shetland*. Edinburgh: 1978.

Fereday, R. P., 'Does Haughty Gaul Invasion Threat?', *Scottish Local History*, Vol. 30, Feb., 1994 & Vol. 31, June, 1994.

Hewison, W. S., 'Holm Farm Diary', *Orkney Miscellany*, Vol. II, 1954.

Hossack, B. H., *Kirkwall in the Orkneys*. Kirkwall: 1900.

Macintosh, W. R., *The Orkney Crofters: Their Evidence and Statements by Agents, as given before the Crofters' Commission*. Kirkwall: 1889.

Miller, Ronald, (ed.), *The Third Statistical Account of Scotland: The County of Orkney*. Edinburgh: 1985.

Omond, James, *Orkney Eighty Years Ago*. Kirkwall: 1911.

Pringle, Robert O., 'On the Agriculture of the Islands of Orkney', *Transactions of the Highlands and Agriculture Society of Scotland*. Edinburgh: 1874.

Shirreff, John, *General View on the Agriculture of the Orkney Islands with Observations on the Means of their Improvement*.

Edinburgh: 1814.

Schrank, Gilbert, 'Crossroad of the North: Proto-Industrialization in the Orkney Islands, 1730–1840'. *The Journal of European Economic History*, Vol. 21. 2, No. 2, 1992.

The Statistical Account of Scotland. Orkney. 1798. Reprinted Wakefield: 1978 (known as Old Statistical Account).

The Statistical Account of the Orkney Islands by the Ministers of their Respective Parishes. Edinburgh: 1842 (known as the New Statistical Account).

Sutherland Graeme, Patrick Neale, *Orkney and the Last Great War: Being Excerpts from the Correspondence of Admiral Alexander Graeme of Graemeshall, 1788–1815*. Kirkwall: 1915.

Sutherland Graeme, Patrick Neale, '*Pateas Amicis*': *The Story of the House of Graemeshall in Orkney*. Kirkwall: 1936.

Thomson, W. P. L., 'Common Land in Orkney', *Orkney Heritage* Vol. 1, 1981.

Thomson, W. P. L., *Kelp-Making in Orkney*. Kirkwall: 1983.

Thomson, W. P. L., *The Little General and the Rousay Crofters: Crisis and Conflict on an Orkney Estate*. Edinburgh: 1981.

Thomson, W. P. L., 'Sober and Tractable? The Hudson's Bay Men in their Orkney Context.' 1990. Typescript.

Thomson, W. P. L., *History of Orkney*. Edinburgh: 1987.

Vink, Bart, 'De Ontwikkeling van de Agrarische Bedriffsstructuur in Orkney, 1840–1930.' Unpublished doctoral thesis, Catholic University of Nijmegen, 1983.

Index